Prayer Before Reading

Come, Holy Spirit, fill the hearts of your faithful
And enkindle in them the fire of your love.
Send forth your Spirit and they shall be created,
And you shall renew the face of the earth.

O God, who did instruct the hearts of the faithful
By the light of the Holy Spirit,
Grant us by the same Spirit to have a right judgment
In all things and ever to rejoice in his consolation.
Through Christ our Lord.
Amen.

Did Jesus Have A Last Name?

And **199** other questions from Catholic teenagers

Matthew Pinto & Jason Evert

ASCENSION

West Chester, Pennsylvania

Nihil obstat:	Rev. Msgr. Joseph G. Prior, S.S.L., S.T.D.
	Censor Librorum
	April 3, 2006
Imprimatur:	+Justin Cardinal Rigali
	Archbishop of Philadelphia
	May 12, 2006

Ascension Press
Post Office Box 1990
West Chester, PA 19380
1-800-376-0520
AscensionPress.com

Cover design: Kinsey Caruth

Printed in the United States of America

ISBN: 978-1-932645-41-5

To all youth leaders, whose commitment to our youth is an extraordinary gift to the Church. Keep up the great work. Your efforts are vital to the future of our culture.

Contents

Publisher's Note

Those of you who are familiar with our previous book for teens, the best-selling *Did Adam & Eve Have Belly Buttons?*, know that its 200 questions are *real* questions from *real* teens. The name and age of the teen who asked a particular question appears next to it, and nearly every question is reproduced practically word-for-word, just as the teen asked it.

Building on the successful formula of its predecessor, *Did Jesus Have a Last Name?* also answers *real* questions from *real* teens. While most appear just as a teen asked them, some are restatements of actual questions asked by teens at conferences attended by one of the authors. As a result, we chose not to include the names and ages of the questioners in this book as we did in *Adam and Eve*.

Introduction

I think teens today are more sophisticated than those of the past. And this is because you've been forced to be. Our media culture exposes you to more of life and the world in a way not possible in past generations. Television, movies, music, and the Internet send constant streams of information into your heads, much of which is negative and contrary to what is best for you.

As a former youth minister, I know firsthand that being a teenager is not easy. All those pressures—from your peers, your parents, your teachers—and all those expectations. Frankly, I think it's probably tougher being a teenager today than at any time in history. Sure, until the twentieth century, people usually got married and started having children in their late teenage years. And many teens worked full time to help support their families. But these kinds of challenges were not as difficult as the mental, moral, and spiritual challenges faced by teens today.

So what's a teen to do?

Well, one thing is for sure—you need to have a firm grounding in your Catholic faith. Just as a tree can survive a hurricane if it has deep roots in the ground, you can survive life's challenges if you build your life on the foundation of Jesus and his teachings.

Here's the logic: If God doesn't exist, then "faith" is meaningless; it's merely a crutch to help you in times of trouble, or just a system of ethics that can and will change over time, depending on circumstances. If, however, God does exist, then his words and wisdom will help us in amazing ways. In fact, if God exists, then living a life he is not involved in is a crazy thing to do. It would be like being an heir to a great fortune and choosing to live the life of a homeless person.

This book was written to help give you a greater certainty that God exists, that he loves you, and that his truth will lead you to peace and happiness. Armed with God's truth, you can achieve greatness, both here on earth and, more importantly, in heaven. You can discover your purpose in life (and likely save yourself a lot of pain in the process).

Did Jesus Have a Last Name? contains two hundred questions about God, morality, Jesus, and a host of things about the church he founded, the Catholic Church. In 1998, when I wrote *Did Adam & Eve Have Belly Buttons?*, I had no idea of the groundswell of interest the book would generate. Teens (along with their parents and teachers) from around the world wrote to me expressing their thanks for answering many of the questions about the Catholic Faith that were on their minds. It became clear that a follow-up book was needed to answer another round of insightful questions from teens. This is where my friend Jason Evert enters the picture.

Jason is a world-class Catholic teacher and speaker. In fact, he is one of the most traveled Catholic youth speakers in the world today, touching the lives of tens of thousands of teenagers each year. Although well-known for his excellent talks on chastity, Jason is primarily a Catholic "apologist," a highly-skilled—yet always charitable— defender of the Faith.

Instead of writing two separate question-and-answer books, Jason and I decided to team up and create a single work through our combined efforts. As the saying goes, "Two heads are better than one." So we each gathered more than a hundred of the most intriguing, relevant, and important questions we have been asked by teens, answered them, and then combined them to create this book. We think you'll like what you find.

We wish you the best as you begin. Be assured that you are in our prayers. We ask for yours as well. If you have more questions, feel free to write or email us. We want to support your search for the truth. It is truly the greatest trip you can ever take.

—Matthew Pinto

Key to Biblical Abbreviations

The following abbreviations are used for the various scriptural verses cited throughout this book. (*Note*: CCC = *Catechism of the Catholic Church*.)

Old Testament

Gn	Genesis	Jon	Jonah
Ex	Exodus	Mi	Micah
Lv	Leviticus	Na	Nahum
Nm	Numbers	Hb	Habakkuk
Dt	Deuteronomy	Zep	Zephaniah
Jos	Joshua	Hg	Haggai
Jgs	Judges	Zec	Zechariah
Ru	Ruth	Mal	Malachi
1 Sam	1 Samuel		
2 Sam	2 Samuel		
1 Kgs	1 Kings		**New Testament**
2 Kgs	2 Kings	Mt	Matthew
1 Chr	1 Chronicles 2	Mk	Mark
Chr	2 Chronicles	Lk	Luke
Ezr	Ezra	Jn	John
Neh	Nehemiah	Acts	Acts
Tb	Tobit	Rom	Romans
Jdt	Judith	1 Cor	1 Corinthians
Est	Esther	2 Cor	2 Corinthians
1 Mc	1 Maccabees	Gal	Galatians
2 Mc	2 Maccabees	Eph	Ephesians
Jb	Job	Phil	Philippians
Ps	Psalms	Col	Colossians
Prv	Proverbs	1 Thess	1 Thessalonians
Eccl	Ecclesiastes	2 Thess	2 Thessalonians
Sng	Song of Songs	1 Tm	1 Timothy
Wis	Wisdom	2 Tm	2 Timothy
Sir	Sirach	Ti	Titus
Is	Isaiah	Phlm	Philemon
Jer	Jeremiah	Heb	Hebrews
Lam	Lamentations	Jas	James
Bar	Baruch	1 Pt	1 Peter
Ez	Ezekiel	2 Pt	2 Peter
Dn	Daniel	1 Jn	1 John
Hos	Hosea	2 Jn	2 John
Jl	Joel	3 Jn	3 John
Am	Amos	Jude	Jude
Ob	Obadiah	Rv	Revelation

Chapter 1

GOD

Question #1

"Who is God and where did he come from?"

A. God is the Creator and Ruler of the universe. He is infinitely above anything we can fully know or comprehend. In the words of the Psalm 145, "God's greatness is unsearchable" (verse 3). But God is also close to us. He is not some abstract, impersonal "Force" that merely created the universe and then went away to let it function on its own. Actually, God holds the entire universe—including you and me—in existence. Without his sustaining power, we would vanish into nothing. As St. Paul puts it, "In him we live and move and have our being" (Acts 17:26-28).

God desires to share his life with us. To accomplish this, he revealed something of the mystery of who he is. To the Israelites, God revealed himself as the one true God (see Dt 6:4-5). At the burning bush on Mount Sinai, God told Moses his name, *Yahweh*, meaning "I AM WHO AM" (Ex 3:13–15), and promised he would save his people from slavery. Jesus revealed the mystery of the Trinity—one God in three Persons: Father, Son, and Holy Spirit (see CCC 232–260).

God possesses many attributes or distinctive qualities that also tell us something of who he is: His *omnipotence* (being all-powerful) tells us the most about him, "For God who created everything, also rules everything and can do everything" (CCC 268). Jesus reveals to us that God is our *loving Father* who takes care of his children. He is merciful and compassionate, and he reveals his almighty power above everything else in the forgiveness of our sins.

Ultimately, God is *Truth* and *Love*. He is the God who can neither deceive nor be deceived. As Psalm 33 says, "For the LORD's Word is true; all his works are trustworthy" (Ps 33:4). The apostle John teaches us that "God is love" (1 Jn 4:8, 16). God's very being is love. The highest expression of his love is shown in the person of Jesus, for "God so loved the world that he gave his only Son, that whoever believes in him may not perish but have eternal life" (Jn 3:16).

God didn't "come from" anywhere. He is pure spirit and therefore does not occupy space like material things do. God is not limited by space or time. He is *eternal*—which means he exists outside of time. He always has been and always will be. Since time is a measurement of change, God is *immutable*—i.e., he does not change—because he exists outside of space and time. For God, all things are eternally present.

Question #2

"Is God also 'Buddha,' 'Allah,' or 'the Holy Spirit'?"

A. To answer this question correctly, we need to look at each of these three names separately.

The name *Buddha* is the honorary title of Siddhartha Gautama, an Indian philosopher of the late sixth and early fifth centuries BC (The word *buddha* means "enlightened one" in Sanskrit.) He taught a system of philosophy and ethics that later became known as Buddhism. But neither Buddha himself nor Buddhists ever considered him divine; he was just a man who taught a new philosophy of life.

Allah is simply the Arabic name for God used by Muslims and some Christians in Arabic-speaking countries. The name Allah acknowledges recognition of the one God, who Muslims also believe revealed himself to Abraham, "the father of all who believe" (Rom 4:11; CCC 146, 841). However, while there are similarities between what Christians, Jews, and Muslims believe about God, there are also many differences. So we should not fall for the modern fallacy that all religions are the same.

Christians believe that God is a *Trinity*—Father, Son, and Holy Spirit—each of whom is God, whole and entire (see CCC 253). As the Third Person of the Blessed Trinity, the Holy Spirit is fully God and equal to the Father and the Son. We acknowledge this truth every Sunday when we proclaim in the Creed, "With the Father and the Son he is worshiped and glorified."

Question #3
"Is God a man or a woman?"

A. As a pure spirit, God does not possess the physical traits of gender; he is neither male nor female (see CCC 370). However, God has revealed himself as "Father." Throughout the Gospels, Jesus speaks of his Father in heaven—for example, "All things have been given to me by my Father" (Mt 11:27). Throughout the Bible, we find masculine pronouns used for God (he, him, his) because they help to communicate the relationship that exists between God our Father and us, "who are under his loving protection" (CCC 238). By calling God "Father," though, we are not implying that men are somehow superior to women.

In the Bible, God's parental tenderness is sometimes expressed by the *image* of motherhood: "As a mother comforts her son, so I will comfort you" (Is 66:13; see CCC 239). However, this verse (along with other similar passages) describes *qualities* of God that can be likened to those of a human mother; nowhere in the Bible, though, is God referred to as "mother." Therefore, calling God "mother" or "she" is inappropriate and contrary to the clear teaching of both Catholic Tradition and Sacred Scripture.

The *Catechism* sums it up in this way: "We ought therefore recall that God transcends the human distinction between the sexes. He is neither man nor woman: he is God. He also transcends human fatherhood and motherhood, although he is their origin and standard: no one is father as God is Father" (CCC 239).

It is important to remember that God *became man* when Jesus took on our humanity and was born into this world. He lived on earth for roughly thirty-three years before dying, rising, and ascending back into heaven. Jesus, even though he now reigns at the right hand of the Father in heaven, still remains *fully God* and *fully man*. Only in this sense, when speaking about Jesus Christ, can we say that God is a man.

Question #4

"Could you give a quick explanation of the Holy Trinity?"

A. The Trinity is "the central mystery of Christian faith and life ... the mystery of God [himself]" (CCC 234). The Trinity could never have been known by human reason;

it had to be revealed to us by God through the person of Jesus.

In the Old Testament, the Israelites understood God to be one: "Hear O Israel: the LORD our God is one LORD" (Dt 6:4). When we say God is one, we are saying he is complete and unchangeable, one in his essence, being, and substance. However, God is also a communion of persons: *Father, Son, and Holy Spirit.* Although there are three Persons, there is one common, divine nature which each Person fully possesses.

The Trinity is a communion of love. The Father loves the Son and the Son loves the Father in return. The love between them is the very person of the Holy Spirit. God invites each of us to share in this communion between the Father and the Son in their Spirit of love (see CCC 850).

Question #5

"How is the Holy Spirit different from God the Father and Jesus?"

A. When we talk about the distinctions between the three Persons of the Trinity, we first have to remember their *unity* as God. The *Catechism* reminds us that "we do not confess three Gods, but one God in three persons" (CCC 253, 256). However, while they are one in their divine *nature,* they are also distinct in their relationships to one another. For example, we know from the Nicene Creed that it is the Son who is "eternally begotten of the Father," and it is the Holy Spirit "who proceeds from the Father and the Son."

The life and work of the Trinity is common to all three Persons: "Inseparable in what they are, the divine Persons are also inseparable in what they do" (CCC 267). For example, we often speak of God the Father as Creator, and this is fine, but the Bible also refers to Jesus, the "Word of God," as creating: "All things were made through him, and without him was not anything made that was made" (Jn 1:3). We may speak of God the Son as Redeemer and God the Holy Spirit as Sanctifier, but it is important to remember that these other names (Creator, Redeemer, Sanctifier) do not define *who* the Persons of the Trinity are. They just represent our own attempt to better understand each Person. In this way, we get a hint about how deep a mystery the Trinity is. St. Thomas Aquinas, one of the Church's most brilliant theologians, said that we can say more about what God is *not* than what he *is!*

However, drawing from Scripture and from theologians like St. Thomas, the Church does help us learn more about each Person of the Trinity, including specifics about the Holy Spirit.

Jesus promised the apostles the gift of the Holy Spirit who descended upon them at Pentecost (as he does for us at baptism and confirmation). It is the Holy Spirit who completes Jesus' work on earth and brings us the fullness of grace (see CCC 2818). "Through his grace, the Holy Spirit is the first to awaken faith in us and to communicate to us the new life which is to 'know the Father and the one whom he sent, Jesus Christ'" (CCC 684; Jn 17:3). Before we can know Christ, we must first be touched by the Holy Spirit who comes to meet us and inspire faith in us, especially in the sacraments (see CCC 683).

Question #6

"What does the Holy Spirit do?"

A. As we proclaim in the Creed, the Holy Spirit is "the Lord, the giver of life." It was through the overshadowing of Mary by the Holy Spirit that Jesus, the only Son of God, was born into the world (see Lk 1:35). It is the Holy Spirit who is at work throughout salvation history. It was the Spirit who led the Israelites through the desert in the form of a cloud and fire (see Ex 40:36-38); whose "finger" wrote the Ten Commandments upon stone tablets (see Ex 31:18); who was symbolized by the dove that Noah released after the Great Flood, through which dry land was found (see Gn 8:8-12); and who descended upon Jesus like a dove at his baptism and remained with him (see Mt 3:16). At Pentecost, the same Spirit rested upon the disciples as "tongues of fire" and filled them with himself in order to lead them "into all truth" (Acts 2:3-4; Jn 14:16-17; CCC 696–701).

It is the Holy Spirit who inspired the writers of Sacred Scripture. He is at work in the teachings of the Church; he brings us into communion with Christ, most especially through the sacraments; he intercedes for us through our prayer; and he is at work in the ministries and missionary life of the Church. By virtue of our baptism, it is the Spirit who dwells within each of us, inviting us to grow in holiness. He transforms us through sanctifying grace and the gifts he offers us. He is our "Advocate" and source of strength on our journey toward heaven (see Jn 14:16, 26; 15:26; 16:7; CCC 688).

Question #7

"Belief in an invisible God makes about as much sense as believing in Santa Claus. How can you believe in a God you can't see?"

A. Most people don't believe in Santa Claus, and it's not because they haven't seen him. They don't believe in him because the evidence shows that he doesn't exist. But this is not the case with God.

The fact that we cannot see God is no proof against his existence. Think about it: There are many things we know exist that we can't see. Have you ever seen a *molecule* or *electricity* or an *idea* or an *emotion* (e.g., love or happiness)? But we know that they exist nonetheless.

Although we can't see these things, we don't doubt their existence, because we experience them all the time. We can't see the wind, but we know it exists because we see its effects in the world: We feel it on our faces and we see trees and objects sway. It is similar with God— we know he exists by his effects on the world and in our lives. Jesus knew we would ask such questions when he said, "Blessed are those who have not seen and yet believe" (Jn 20:29).

Yet, in a very profound way, we *can* see God—in the person and life of Jesus, the God-man, the Second Person of the Trinity. As St. Paul puts it, Jesus is "the image of the invisible God" (Col 1:15). Jesus assures us that "he who has seen me has seen the Father" (Jn 14: 9). Upon his ascension into heaven, Jesus promised that he would remain with us forever through the Church (see Mt 28:20). Through faith, Christ is made visible to us within his Church: "The Church is the Body of Christ. Through the Spirit and his action in the sacraments, above all the Eucharist, Christ, who once was dead and is now risen, establishes the community of believers as his own Body" (CCC 805).

Question #8

"An agnostic friend of mine asked me to show her proof of God's existence without using the Bible as part of my argument. What should I say?"

A. Many ancient philosophers—Plato and Aristotle, for example—developed arguments for the existence of God based entirely on reason. In addition, the Church has consistently taught that the existence of God can be known with certainty by natural reason (see CCC 50).

Some of this solid reasoning can be seen in St. Thomas Aquinas' "proofs" for the existence of God. In one of these proofs, St. Thomas observed that all created things rely on something outside of themselves for their own existence (e.g., each person relies on his or her parents). However, he also recognized the necessity of a being whose existence does *not* rely on something outside of itself. Otherwise, nothing could exist. We refer to this uncreated being, or *uncaused cause*, as God (see CCC 31–35).[1] In all, St. Thomas offered five proofs or "ways" to know of God's existence. There is a great book called *A Tour of the Summa* (TAN Books, 1978) that offers a short summary of these proofs. You may want to examine all of them for yourself.

Finally, as much as our reasoning power can assure us of God's existence, it is only when God reveals himself to us that we can truly know him. God's full revelation is communicated to us through Sacred Scripture and Sacred Tradition under the guidance and direction of the Church (see CCC 84–87).

Question #9

"If God can do anything, then is it possible for him to make a rock so big that he can't lift it?"

A. The problem here is with the question itself. God actually can't "do anything" that would contradict his nature. For example, he cannot do evil. So the question itself is illogical. This question is intended to trick the person who hears it into thinking he is stuck in a corner. However, in reality, the person who asks illogical questions like this one is actually tricking himself by using bad logic and faulty reasoning, which naturally leads to confusion.

This is what we mean: Let's imagine for a moment that God created something "indestructible" and then destroyed it. Was it ever indestructible to begin with? No. The idea of destroying an indestructible object is like trying to make a square circle—it is a contradiction in terms. While God can always do things that *surpass* our reason, he can never *contradict* reason; he is the God of truth and can neither deceive nor be deceived.

Question #10

"If God is all-powerful and all loving, then why does he allow suffering and evil to exist in the world?"

A. God created our first parents, Adam and Eve, free from suffering. They walked in friendship with God and in harmony with each other and the created world. This state of original holiness and justice allowed God's sanctifying grace to penetrate their very beings (see CCC 375). However, through sin, our first parents chose to break this intimate union with God. In doing so, they lost God's grace and thus became subject to suffering and death (see CCC 400). As a result, evil entered the world.

Suffering and evil, therefore, are direct consequences of sin. Though God is not the cause of evil, he *permits* it because he respects our freedom and, in a mysterious way, knows how to derive good from it (CCC 311). God created each of us with free will, which allows us to make our own choices in life (otherwise, we would not be human). Even though we may sometimes abuse that freedom and stray from God, he will never stray from us. Because he loves us and knows what is best for us, he never ceases calling us to himself. In part, he permits suffering as a way of gaining our attention and reminding us of our complete dependence upon him. Ultimately, God permits suffering in order to help us grow in faith and in our love for him and each other.

In everyday life, we can distinguish *moral evil* and *physical evil*. Moral evil is the result of a human action that goes against the divine or natural law of God—in other words, sin (see CCC 311). Sin brings about much of the pain we suffer, either directly or indirectly. But not all suffering we experience is the result of our personal sins. Much physical evil—such as diseases and natural disasters—is simply the result of us living in a fallen world (see CCC 310).

In his great mercy, God did not leave man abandoned to the power of death. He sent us a Savior, Jesus, who made amends for the disobedience of Adam by conquering sin and death through his own suffering on a cross (see 1 Cor 15:21–22, 45; Phil 2:8; Rom 5:19-20; CCC 312). It is *through* enduring evil and suffering that Christ gains victory over sin and death, thus restoring man's friendship with God.

Although Jesus accomplished our salvation once-and-for-all through his suffering and death on the Cross, we must freely accept God's invitation to love him and to share the earthly lot of the saints and martyrs who now are face to face with him in heaven. This is what St. Paul means when he says, "Now I rejoice in my sufferings for your sake, and in my flesh I complete what is lacking in Christ's afflictions" (Col 1:24). Our purpose on earth, as followers of Jesus, is to imitate him in our lives. Jesus himself tells us that this will be difficult and involve suffering: "If any man would come after me, let him deny himself and take up his cross daily and follow me" (Lk 9:23) and, "Whoever does not bear his own cross and come after me, cannot be my disciple" (Lk 14:27).

In a beautiful way, then, we should join our sufferings to Jesus' sufferings and offer them up to God. When we do so, they become redemptive not only for us, but for the salvation of others and the whole world. As St. Paul tells us in his letter to the Romans, "We know that in everything God works for good with those who love him, who are called according to his purpose" (Rom 8:28).

Question #11

"If God knows everything, then he knows whether we're going to end up in heaven or hell. Doesn't this take away our free will, since we can't change what God already knows will happen?"

A. Just because God *knows* where we will end up—heaven or hell—this does not mean he *causes* us to go to either place. Remember: God is eternal; he is not restricted by time like we are. For God, there is no such thing as past, present, or future, but only "now." This is difficult to understand, so here's an analogy that might help.

Think of a man sitting on top of a tall building looking down upon a city. From his vantage point he is able to witness events as they occur. At one point, he notices two cars speeding, about to collide at an intersection. Neither of the drivers is aware of the other car because they can't see each other. Does the knowledge of the man on the building in any way restrict the freedom of the two drivers? Of course not. Both drivers could choose to slow down immediately and obey the rules of the road. Although God's presence in our lives is much different from the way a man watches the world from a building, the analogy does help us understand that even though God knows the outcome of all things, he will never remove our free will in our choosing to either love him or reject him. In fact, without that freedom, you and I would never have the ability to choose to follow Christ in order to attain heaven. "Men, as intelligent and free creatures, have to journey toward their ultimate destinies by their free choice and preferential love" (CCC 311).

Question #12

"In the *Our Father,* we pray, 'Lead us not into temptation.' I thought Satan was the one who tempts us. Does God tempt us to sin, too?"

A. No, God does not tempt us to sin. The original Greek of the New Testament is sometimes difficult to translate precisely into English. The word "lead" here is a good example of this. The original Greek phrase combines the ideas of "do not allow us to *enter into* temptation" and "do not let us *yield* [give in] to temptation." So, the idea of God tempting us to sin is not meant here. Actually, we are asking him not to allow us to choose a path that may lead us into sin.

But you are right: Satan is the one who tempts us. As St. Ambrose says, "It is God who protects [us] and keeps [us] from the wiles of … the devil, so that the enemy, who is accustomed to leading into sin, may not surprise [us]. One who entrusts himself to God does not [fear] the devil" (CCC 2852).[2]

Though we may struggle to overcome certain sins, God is always ready to give us the grace to resist temptation. So we can never say "the devil made me do it." No one— including the devil—can make us sin; it is our choice. As St. Paul tells us, "No testing has overtaken you that is not common to man. God is faithful, and he will not let you be tempted beyond your strength, but with temptation will also provide the way of escape, so that you may be able to endure it" (1 Cor 10:13). In a way, when we pray the *Our Father,* we are asking God to show us the way to the escape that Scripture says he will provide for us.

Question #13

"How do I know that God will always be there for me?"

A. You can know that God will always be there for you because he said he would—and God always keeps his promises. Throughout the Bible, God constantly reminds us of his presence in our lives. In the Old Testament, God affirms this in a special way: "Before I formed you in the womb I knew you, and before you were born I consecrated you" (Jer 1:5); "can a mother forget her infant, be without tenderness for the child of her womb? … Even should she forget, I will never forget you" (Is 49:15). Jesus himself reminds us of our value and worth: "Are not five sparrows sold for two pennies? And not one of them is forgotten before God. Even the hairs of your head are all numbered. Fear not, you are of more value than many sparrows" (Lk 12:6-7).

The apostles took great comfort in knowing that Jesus promised he would never abandon them: "I will not leave you [orphans]" (Jn 14:18). Though seated at the right hand of the Father in heaven, Jesus is also present to us in his Church: "For where two or three are gathered in my name, there I am in the midst of them" (Mt 18:20). Through the Holy Spirit, Jesus is made present to us in a special way by priests, who stand in the place of Christ in the celebration of the sacraments. He is present to us in his Word, the Bible. Above all, Jesus is present to us in the Holy Eucharist—his Body, Blood, Soul, and Divinity. It is in the Eucharist that we find Jesus, the One who is true God and true man. All we need to do is go to him and he will fill us with his abundant grace. "And behold, I am with you always, even until the end of time" (Mt 28:20).

Chapter 2

CREATION AND MAN

Question #14

"I've heard there are two Creation stories in Genesis. Why is this?"

A. The book of Genesis has two Creation stories (or *accounts*) in order to emphasize different theological truths. While Christian tradition considers Moses the author of Genesis, some Scripture scholars believe that several "editors" contributed to the book. This may explain the different emphasis given in the two Creation accounts. But remember—if you look closely, neither of the Creation stories contradicts the other in any way. In fact, both offer truths about the origin of the world and of man that complement each other.

The first Creation account emphasizes God's transcendence over his creation. God alone is the supreme master of the universe. Here we learn that man is made in the "image" and "likeness" of God and is given "dominion ... over all the earth" (Gn 1:1-31). In contrast, the second Creation account is more vivid, using imagery and familiar descriptions that make it easy to understand. God is described as having "formed man of dust from the ground, and breathed into his nostrils the breath of life" (Gn 2:7). He is characterized as a gardener, "And out of the ground the LORD God made to grow every tree" (Gn 2:9).

Within this account, Adam and Eve hear "the sound of the LORD God walking in the garden in the cool of the day" (Gn 3:8).

As the inspired Word of God, the Genesis Creation accounts offer us truths about God, man, and the origin of the world that are intended to help us grow in faith. Both offer different perspectives on the same truth: that God created the universe out of love for us, and that we in turn are "created to serve and love God" (CCC 358).

Question #15

"Was the world really created in six days?"

A. This question cannot be answered with a simple "yes" or "no." To understand the Bible correctly we must always read it within the living Tradition of the Church (see CCC 113). Though God inspired the human authors of the Bible, we need to consider the styles of writing, literary types, and ways of speaking that they used (see CCC 110). For example, some parts of the Bible are written as historical narratives (i.e., they discuss events as they actually happened), while other parts are written using a poetic or symbolic style.

With this in mind, let's turn to the source of the Creation story—the book of Genesis. Much of this book is written as history and should be interpreted as such. However, parts of it—particularly its first eleven chapters—are written using symbolic and figurative language. So the author of Genesis didn't intend to provide a detailed, scientific explanation of God's Creation of the universe. At the time Genesis was written, what is now known as scientific knowledge was extremely limited. The author's primary purpose here is to convey *religious*—not scientific—truths about the origins of the world, man, and man's relationship to God in a poetic, symbolic way.

Because the Creation story is written poetically, the human author of Genesis probably did not use the word "day" to mean a literal, twenty-four-hour period. The word "day" may have been used to draw distinctions between the different aspects of God's creative work (e.g., man in comparison to the rest of creation). The author describes Creation as taking place over six days, with God resting on the seventh day (see Gn 1:1-31, 2:1-3). The six days can be understood to represent the order of God's plan for the universe, and to show a rhythm of work and rest that God inscribes in the Jewish law: a blessing of the Sabbath day—a day of rest, dedicated to the LORD.

Question #16
"What area of the world did God create first?"

A. The Bible speaks of God creating the heavens and the earth, separating light from darkness, and dividing water from dry land. And upon the earth, God "put forth vegetation, plants yielding seed, and fruit trees bearing fruit in which is their seed, each according to its kind, upon the earth" (Gn 1:1-11). But the Bible never tells us the exact location of where the Creation of the world began.

The book of Genesis, though, does give us some interesting details about the Garden of Eden. It is described as a place with a river divided into four separate rivers: the Pishon, Gihon, Tigris, and Euphrates (see Gn 2:10-14). The Tigris and Euphrates are the names of two rivers located in present-day Iraq. The region there has been known throughout history as *Mesopotamia* and has within it a large plain referred to as the *Fertile Crescent.* This area was the home to the world's most ancient civilizations, a number of which are mentioned in the Bible: the Babylonians, the Assyrians, and before them, the Chaldeans (or Sumerians) who inhabited Ur, the birthplace of Abraham (see Gn 11:27-32).

Question #17

"If the Church teaches that the Bible—including Genesis—is true, then it must reject evolution, right?"

A. Actually, no. The Church does not reject the *possibility* that God could have created man and the universe through an evolutionary process. God could have infused a human soul into a pre-existent living being, thereby making it a *human* being. This possibility, however, in no way contradicts the Creation accounts found in the book of Genesis, if they are correctly understood. As mentioned earlier, Genesis was not written to offer a scientific explanation of God's Creation of the world and man. Instead, the author of Genesis is more interested in conveying *religious* truths that deal directly with God's purpose in creating the world, as well as man's place in it.

The Church teaches that everything owes its existence to God (see CCC 338). Whether he created the universe through a process of evolution or by some other means is of secondary importance. Concerning the origin of the world, we must affirm the following:

1. God created the universe *ex nihilo,* "out of nothing" (CCC 296).

2. Everything he created is good (see CCC 299).

3. Man was created in God's image and likeness (Gn 1:27; CCC 355).

4. Adam and Eve lost their original state of innocence and holiness through sin (see CCC 399, 405). As a result, death and suffering entered creation (see CCC 400).

5. All human beings inherit this state of original sin (see CCC 402–406).

6. God promised a Savior who would redeem us from our fallen state and lead us to salvation (see CCC 410, 411).

Remember: Evolution is a scientific *theory.* Though often taught as fact, many of its aspects have been challenged by a growing number of scientists simply because the fossil evidence is missing, or even conflicting. Because faith and science both find their origin in God, it stands to reason that scientific theories concerning the origins of the world, as well as religious truths related to them, should be compatible with one another (see CCC 159).

Question #18

"If the Church is infallible, why doesn't it settle the question of Creation and evolution?"

A. As we saw in the previous answer, the Church is mainly concerned with the *why*—not the *how*—of creation. After we acknowledge God as Creator, precisely how human life came about is a matter for science to consider; the Church's principal mission is to teach on matters of faith and morality.

While the Church is indeed infallible when teaching or clarifying the contents of God's revelation, this does not mean that the Church has the ability to make dogmatic pronouncements on every scientific theory. Infallibility does not mean the Church knows everything. There are many things Christ has not revealed to his Church, such as the exact date of his Second Coming, which the Bible says no one but the Father knows (Mt 24:36). Therefore, the Church cannot and will not teach infallibly on matters that have not been revealed to it, including those directly related to the issue of evolution.

Question #19

"Did Adam and Eve really exist? Did they really eat the forbidden fruit, or is this just symbolic?"

A. The Church has always taught that God created a first man (Adam) and a first woman (Eve) in his "image and likeness." The name *Adam* is derived from the Hebrew word for "man," and *Eve* comes from the Hebrew for "life," for it is through her that all human life originates. The *Catechism* tells us that our first parents were created in an original "state of holiness and justice," meaning that they were in friendship with God and were in harmony with each other and creation around them (see CCC 375). As long as they obeyed God, they remained in friendship with him and were free from all suffering and death.

In Genesis, we learn that God gave Adam and Eve the freedom to eat of any tree of the Garden, except one— the "Tree of the Knowledge of Good and Evil" (Gn 2:17). Because the Creation story is written using figurative language, many of its descriptions have a symbolic meaning. For example, the *Catechism* states that the Tree of the Knowledge of Good and Evil "symbolically evokes the insurmountable limits that man, being a creature, must freely recognize and respect with trust. Man is dependent on his Creator and subject to the laws of creation and to the moral norms that govern the use of freedom" (CCC 396).

Furthermore, our first parents' eating of the forbidden fruit symbolizes humanity's disobedience to God's law and thus constitutes our first sin (Gn 3:1-11). Whether the sin of our first parents actually involved a piece of fruit taken from a forbidden tree is really not that important. What *is* important is that Adam and Eve *did* sin, and all of mankind subsequently inherits their fallen state.

You may be interested to know that Genesis never mentions the actual name of the forbidden fruit eaten by Adam and Eve, even though we often hear it was an apple. Don't worry though—I don't think anyone is going to change the name of the protruding part of your throat from "Adam's apple" to "Adam's peach" anytime soon!

Question #20

"Why are we punished for Adam and Eve's sin?"

A. As descendents of Adam and Eve, we are born into original sin. This is not through any fault of our own, but simply because we have inherited our human nature from them. The nature we have inherited is in a fallen condition, negatively affected by the absence of sanctifying grace, lost through Adam's sin. That original sin, though, is not something we have "committed"—it is a "condition" we inherit (see CCC 404).

After our first parents' sin, God did not abandon us to sin and death. He sent his only Son who, through his death on the Cross, not only makes amends for the sin of Adam and of the whole world, but renews all things in himself: "I have come that you may have life, and have it to the full" (Jn 10:10). Therefore, in a most glorious way, Christ's inexpressible grace has given us blessings better than those which sin has taken away from us (see CCC 412, 420). As St. Thomas Aquinas writes, "There is nothing to prevent human nature from being raised up to something greater, even after sin."[3] It is Christ who restores that which was lost through original sin and raises us up to even greater heights by inviting us to share in his very life. This is the reason why baptism is so important. It is the means by which sanctifying grace enters our souls and our friendship with God is restored.

If Adam and Eve had remained faithful to God, their children would have inherited the same nature enjoyed by their parents in the Garden. However, this does not mean they had an exclusive right to that inheritance. Furthermore, if we had also gained that inheritance, I can hardly imagine that we would be complaining about having it *so good,* especially when considering we *did nothing* to deserve it. We should keep this in mind when we compare the sin of Adam and Eve with our own sins and lack of faithfulness to God.

Question #21

"Would Jesus have had to come to die for us if Adam and Eve didn't sin?"

A. The sole reason Jesus came into the world and died on the Cross was to redeem us from the sin of Adam and Eve, as well as all subsequent sins of the whole world. In the words of the *Catechism,* "His redemptive passion was the very reason for his Incarnation" (CCC 607). The *Catechism* also tells us, "we do know by Revelation that Adam had received original holiness and justice not for himself alone, but for all human nature" (CCC 404).

So, even if Adam and Eve had never sinned, we cannot assume that their offspring would not have sinned. Therefore, if Adam and Eve hadn't sinned but one of their offspring did, we still would have needed a Savior. Jesus would have carried out his saving work for even a single sinner, regardless of who it was.

Jesus himself is the Good Shepherd who tells us he would leave his flock of ninety-nine in order to find the one who has gone astray (Lk 15:4-7). "There is not, never has been, and never will be a single human being for whom Christ did not suffer" (CCC 605). If, on the other hand, no human being ever sinned throughout the history of mankind (a pleasant thought indeed), there would have been no reason for Jesus to suffer and die.

Question #22

"Did the dinosaurs come before Adam and Eve or vice versa?"

A. There is some disagreement among scientists over the specific times when certain animals appeared and lived on the earth. Fossil records also give varied indications as to the actual age of man. However, scientists work within a generally accepted geological dating system that divides the history of the world into *eras:* the Paleozoic, Mesozoic, and Cenozoic. According to these divisions, the dinosaurs existed during the Mesozoic Era, which lasted from about 248 to 65 million years ago. (Remember the movie *Jurassic Park?* The Jurassic period occurred during the Mesozoic era.) Man, on the other hand, appeared during the Cenozoic Era and thus did not inhabit the earth until long after the dinosaurs became extinct.

Question #23

"Were Adam and Eve cavemen?"

If you mean, "Could Adam and Eve have lived in a cave?" The answer is, yes, they could have. After their banishment from the Garden of Eden, Adam and Eve certainly needed to provide shelter for themselves and later for their children. It is certainly possible they could have found a cave they particularly liked, placed a "welcome" mat out front, and called it home. On the other hand, if you're asking, "Did Adam and Eve resemble the hunched over, knuckles scraping the ground figure we picture as a 'caveman'?" the answer is certainly no.

The Church teaches that we must affirm that God created man in his own image and likeness. What does this mean? It means that God endowed man with intelligence and a free will. The *Catechism* tells us that, "The human person participates in the light and power of the divine Spirit. By his reason, he is capable of understanding the order of things established by the Creator. By free will, he is capable of directing himself toward his true good" (CCC 1704). The image of God is present in every man. "Endowed with a 'spiritual and immortal' soul, the human person is 'the only creature on earth that God has willed for its own sake.' From his conception, he is destined for eternal beatitude" (CCC 1702–1703). So, while Adam and Eve probably didn't have the same table manners that we have today, they were as fully human as you and me. They were not "cavemen" in the sense of being lesser developed versions of an evolving species that still had some "monkey" to evolve out of their systems!

Question #24

"If Adam and Eve were the only original people, who was Cain's wife? If he married his sister, wouldn't this have been incest and have caused genetic problems in their children?"

A. Cain would have married his sister. At the beginning of time, though, this practice was acceptable in the eyes of God for the obvious reason that the human race could not have continued without it. But we should not see this as a contradiction to God's moral law, i.e., that he makes certain exceptions merely for the sake of convenience. We know today that inbreeding can be a dangerous health hazard. When close blood relatives (people who share a common gene pool) marry, the chance of passing on a lethal gene combination to their children is greatly increased.

The average human being today carries four to six lethal genes. They can be caused by deletions and mutations of genes in the gene structure of the cell, and these lethal genes are what cause problems with inbreeding. However, since Adam and Eve were God's original couple, they would have had the purest genetic code possible. Without such lethal combinations, any danger of genetic mutations among their children (or their children's children) was very unlikely. This helps us understand why God would have *originally* allowed for marriage among the sons and daughters of Adam and Eve (and, indeed, for other Israelites—for example, Abraham, who married his half-sister—until the Law of Moses specifically forbid it.) However, given the health dangers and the moral complications that could result within families that would form such relationships, God eventually prohibited marriage between close relatives, including other degrees of kinship that may be called incestuous (see Lv 18:7-20; CCC 2388).

Question #25

"If Adam and Eve were the only two humans that God created at the beginning, wouldn't that make the entire population of the world a huge extended family?"

A. You're right—we *are* all one huge extended family! As descendants of our first parents, all human beings are related to one another. The *Catechism* tells us we are all of a "common origin ... All nations form but one community. This is so because all stem from the one stock which God created to people the entire earth" (CCC 842).

In recent years, science seems to have confirmed our common human ancestry. There have even been a number of genetic studies conducted that strongly suggest all humans are descended from a single set of parents. One of them, conducted by evolutionary biologists from Yale, Harvard, and the University of Chicago during the early 1990s, looked for genetic differences in the "Y" chromosome of thirty-eight men of different ethnic backgrounds who were living in different parts of the world. Within their research, they discovered particular characteristics common to all the men's "Y" chromosomes. Based on their analysis, they concluded that all thirty-eight had descended from the same original father. This same conclusion was drawn by an American researcher in molecular evolution, Michael Hammer, in a similar research study conducted at about the same time. In addition, a British team of geneticists, while examining a much larger segment of the human "Y" chromosome, also concluded that modern humans all descended from a common male ancestor.

In 1987, *before* the studies described above were conducted, a completely independent study by a team of molecular biologists at the University of California at Berkeley concluded that, based on the genetic evidence, all humans share a common *female* ancestor. The researchers appropriately named her "Eve."[4]

Question #26

"If all of us came from Adam and Eve, then why are there so many different races and ethnic groups?"

A. As we saw in the answer to question #25, recent scientific evidence seems to indicate that the entire human race is descended from one man and one woman. This being so, there is a perfectly natural explanation for how different races could all have come from a single set of parents. For example, think about your own family. Do all of your brothers and sisters look exactly like your parents? Some of them probably resemble one of your parents more than the other. If you consider your extended family (e.g., grandparents, aunts, uncles, cousins, nephews, nieces, etc.), you will probably notice even more differences than similarities. Maybe someone in your family doesn't resemble anybody! The point here is that even within one or two generations of the same family, you will find a wide diversity of traits: different sizes and shapes, eye and hair color, facial features, and skin pigment.

Adam and Eve held within them the genetic material that eventually gave rise to all the various races, just as parents today have the genetic material which results in the physical differences among their children. "The whole human race is in Adam 'as one body of one man'"[5] (CCC 404).

There is enough scientific evidence to suggest that man, after having made his entrance into the world, spread out throughout the earth from a single geographical starting point. The Bible certainly speaks of Noah and his three sons, Shem, Ham, and Japheth, along with their wives; and "from these the nations spread out over the earth after the flood" (Gn 10:32). As particular groups moved to specific regions of the world, they became acclimated to that region, settling there and populating it. Obviously, over the course of countless generations, the people of these regions would come to resemble one another in a distinctive way. Not only that, they would come to develop a common language, culture, and overall way of life. This explains the beautiful and rich diversity of the nations and peoples of the world.

Finally, we need to remember that although we represent various races, colors, and ethnicities, we are all one people. The *Catechism* reminds us that, "Because of its common origin, the human race forms a unity, for 'from one ancestor [God] made all nations to inhabit the whole earth'" (Acts 17:26; Tb 8:6; CCC 360). This unity finds its fulfillment in Jesus, the "light of the nations" and the hope of salvation for all mankind (see Jn 1:4).[6]

Chapter 3

RELIGION AND THE BIBLE

Question #27

"When we say the Bible is God's Word, does that mean that God actually wrote it? Didn't he use men to write it?"

A. Actually, you're right on both counts. As the *Catechism* tells us, God *is* the author of the Bible (CCC 105). But he chose certain men to actually write the books of the Old and New Testaments under the inspiration of the Holy Spirit. During the first three centuries AD, the Church discerned which writings were inspired by the Holy Spirit and included them within the list (called the *canon*) of sacred books.

Regarding the writing of these sacred texts, the *Catechism* states that God "made full use of [the human writers'] faculties and powers so that, though he acted in them and by them, it was as true authors that they consigned to write whatever he wanted written and no more" (CCC 106). In other words, God did not dictate the words of Sacred Scripture to the human writers nor did he temporarily suspend their free will, style of writing, emotions, intellect, or cultural influences. Rather, God worked within and through the natural abilities of the human writers in order to speak to us "in a human way." When we read the Bible, "we must be attentive to what the human authors truly wanted to affirm and to what God wanted to reveal to us by their words" (CCC 109). Rather than diminishing the freedom of the human author in the composition of Sacred Scripture, God enhanced that freedom. Within that freedom, an authentic openness to the inspiration of the Holy Spirit was exercised, allowing the human author to become the very instrument by which God's written Word is conveyed to us.

St. Teresa of Calcutta (Mother Teresa) used to encourage her sisters to be "a pencil" in the hand of God, allowing him to write whatever message he wanted with their lives. In a sense, the human writers of the Bible were "pencils" in the hand of God, humbly allowing him to use their unique gifts and circumstances through which he could perfectly write his message of love to us.

Question #28

"After two thousand years, how do we know that the Bible we have today is the same one that the first Christians used?"

A. From the time of the apostles to now, it has been the Church's highest priority to faithfully preserve and protect the Faith entrusted to it by Jesus himself. In the New Testament, Paul implores Timothy to guard and keep safe the deposit of faith which has been entrusted to him (see 1 Tm 6:20). For two thousand years, millions of Christians have given their very lives in defense of the Faith. It is integral to the Church's mission to uphold the integrity of the Faith in both its written form—Sacred Scripture—and proclaimed Word—Sacred Tradition. This is why St. Paul also tells the Thessalonians to "hold to the traditions which you were taught by us, either by word of mouth or by letter" (2 Thess 2:15).

It was the Church, under the guidance of the Holy Spirit, which finally determined which books were to be included in the sacred canon (i.e., the list of inspired books) of the Bible. This process took three centuries and was ultimately resolved at the Council of Hippo in AD 393. Later, at the Councils of Carthage in both AD 397 and 419, the universal Church continued the process and finally determined which books were divinely inspired and which were not.

The earliest Christians did not have access to the Bible in the way that we do today. The first printed Bible was not available until the printing press was invented in the fifteenth century, and even then, the number of copies was very limited and not affordable for most people. Christians who lived during the first centuries after Christ had to rely almost exclusively on the proclaimed Word of God (i.e., Sacred Tradition), as taught by the apostles and their immediate successors. Although the books of the Hebrew Old Testament were well-known and firmly established during the time of the early Church, the first New Testament books were not written until about AD 50 when St. Paul began writing his letters to the various Christian communities. The Gospels followed later. The book of Revelation, the final book of the Bible, was not written by St. John until about AD 90.

Unfortunately, no *autographs* (i.e., original manuscripts) of any biblical books have survived until today. This is not surprising, given that they were written thousands of years ago on parchment and papyrus, which both decay over time. In addition, many manuscripts of the Bible were ordered destroyed during times of persecution by the Roman emperors. The oldest known existing manuscript of a portion of the Bible is the Dead Sea

Scrolls, discovered in a cave near Jericho in 1947. Written in Hebrew by a Jewish community living in that region around the second century AD, it contains portions of most of the books of the Old Testament as well as a complete text of the book of Isaiah. It closely matches the version of the text we have now.

The oldest known existing fragment of the Bible written in Greek, the original language of the New Testament, can be dated to the second century AD. Many other Greek manuscripts have also been discovered over the years. Of those, perhaps the most important and complete, as well as the oldest, is known as the *Codex Vaticanus*. Dated approximately AD 325, it offers one of the most accurate and reliable witnesses of the Bible's original texts known to exist. Today, it is safely preserved in the Vatican Library.

In about AD 400, St. Jerome was commissioned by Pope Damasus to translate the Bible from its original languages (Hebrew, Aramaic, and Greek) into Latin. This version is known as the *Vulgate*, a word meaning the "common" Latin of the day. As the various European languages developed, the Bible was translated by hand from the Vulgate into these languages.

Although it was recently revised, the Vulgate remains the official Latin translation recognized by the Catholic Church. Since the Second Vatican Council (1962–1965), however, the Church has encouraged newer translations of the Bible directly from the original languages. This scholarly effort has resulted in a number of new Catholic Bible translations, including the *New American Bible*, which is used during Mass. Another excellent translation is the *Revised Standard Version–Catholic Edition*, which is used in the *Catechism*.

Catholics should make sure any Bible they use has an *Imprimatur* (i.e., an official declaration of a bishop that its text is free from doctrinal error).

In this way, the Church continues to be the official guardian and infallible interpreter of the Word of God. So we can be assured that God's revelation, as given to the apostles by Christ himself and preserved throughout the years by the Church in both Sacred Scripture and Tradition, is the same today as it was at the time of the first Christians.

Question #29

"How can we know the Bible is accurate?"

A. We know the Bible is accurate—that it is without error in matters of faith and morality—because God is its principal Author. Otherwise, we would be implying that God is fallible or is somehow trying to deceive us. This, of course, is impossible because God is Truth itself. As the psalmist says, "The sum of your word is truth, and every one of your righteous ordinances endures forever" (Ps 119:160). We find similar words in the second book of Samuel, "And now O LORD God, you are God, and your words are true" (2 Sam 7:28; CCC 215).

If you're asking, "How do we know that the actual words of the Bible today are the same as the original text?" then that's a different matter. Here we need the science of *textual criticism,* the method biblical scholars use to examine the various copies of the books of the Bible and to determine the original text.

Experts place a lot of weight on finding copies of books and also on the time gap between the originals

and the dating of the earliest copies. Scripture scholar
F.F. Bruce, in his book *New Testament Documents: Are
They Reliable?* (InterVarsity Press, 1982), argues that
there is far more evidence for the accuracy of the New
Testament than for other well-accepted works of classical
history. For example, the Roman historian, Tacitus, lived
and chronicled events at the end of the first century, but
the earliest copies of his works date from *one thousand
years later.* Only about twenty copies exist today. Another
example is Julius Caesar's commentaries on the Gallic
Wars (58–50 BC). The earliest copies of this work that have
been found date roughly *950 years later* (AD 900), and
only about ten copies are in existence. Yet no respected
scholar questions the authenticity of these works.

What about the Old and New Testaments, which were
completely written by AD 100? The Dead Sea Scrolls,
which were discovered in 1947, include complete copies
of the Old Testament, dating from the first and second
centuries. By the middle of the fourth century, more than
five thousand Greek copies, ten thousand Latin copies,
and nine thousand other copies of the complete New
Testament existed!

One of the most important documents of Vatican II tells
us that "since everything asserted by the inspired author
or sacred writer must be held to be asserted by the Holy
Spirit, it follows that the books of Scripture must be
acknowledged as teaching *solidly, faithfully,* and *without
error* that truth which God wanted put into sacred
writings for the sake of salvation."[7] So we should feel
confident in proclaiming that the Bible is not only reliable,
it is *inerrant* (i.e., without error) on matters of faith and
morality because it has God as its Author.

Question #30

"A friend of mine mentioned that the Bible was written a long time ago and its teachings—especially on sex—are not relevant today. How do I explain that God's laws are the same always?"

A. It is important to recognize that God's laws are eternal because he is eternal. If we truly believe that God created us out of love, then we should trust that he knows what is good for us. All the laws he has given are to help us, to protect us from what he knows is not good for us. The same is true for our own society, and this is why our government says it is illegal to go 160 MPH on the interstate. This law helps us from hurting ourselves and others.

God's laws are the same when it comes to sex. God created us, God created sex, and God created marriage—and he made them to go together. He knows how they should be used in order to bring us happiness. This is why God teaches us that sex belongs within marriage. Our culture may look and act differently than the societies living when God gave us these laws. However, the human race has remained essentially the same. We are people made in God's image and likeness. We have dignity. We still need food, shelter, and water. And sex is still a major part of our lives, otherwise we would not exist! Human nature is the same today as it was for Adam and Eve, who were just as attracted to the opposite sex as we are. This explains why God's laws, including those about sex, are as relevant for us today as they were during the time of Moses.

When we arbitrarily decide which of God's laws we will no longer follow, we embark on a path that will eventually lead to our ruin. As the *Catechism* wisely reminds us, "The way of Christ 'leads to life'; a contrary way 'leads to destruction'" (Mt 7:13; see Dt 30:15-20). As the *Catechism* puts it, "The Gospel ... shows the importance of moral decisions for our salvation; 'There are two ways, the one of life, the other of death; but between the two, there is a great difference'" (CCC 1696).

Question #31

"Aren't there contradictions in the Bible, for example, about how Judas died? How can the Church say the Bible has no errors?"

A. Many apparent contradictions in the Bible actually are not, if they are understood correctly. The death of Judas is a good example of this fact. The two accounts of Judas' death are Matthew 27:5, which tells us that he "hanged himself," and Acts 1:18, which describes Judas as "falling headlong, he burst open in the middle, and all his insides spilled out." It is clear that neither account contradicts the other; each offers different details—a different *perspective*—on the same event. Both authors want to express the depth of despair that Judas experienced, hence the graphic descriptions of his death. The particulars may not be exactly the same, but the underlying event *is* the same.

So, it is entirely possible that, when he hanged himself (as Matthew describes) the noose broke and he fell to the ground. From this point, Luke's description can be seen as entirely compatible with Matthew's; it is not contradictory at all. In fact, this is exactly how the two accounts are blended together in the classic 1960s movie about Jesus, *King of Kings.*

Question #32

"In the Old Testament, the penalty for adultery was death. In the Gospel, though, Jesus forgave the woman caught in adultery. Does this mean that morality is different in the Old and New Testaments?"

A. No. The Church has always upheld the *unity* of the divine plan found in the Old and New Testaments (CCC 128). In other words, there is only one Word of God given to us over the course of thousands of years, involving several generations of God's people. The *Catechism* describes this as a "dynamic movement toward the fulfillment of the divine plan when 'God will be everything to everyone'" (1 Cor 15:28; CCC 130). That fulfillment was reached in the person of Christ. This helps us recognize that the value and authority of the Old Testament is not diminished because of Jesus' coming—it is actually reaffirmed and strengthened (see CCC 129).

So the moral law of the New Testament is the same as in the Old. In the example you mention, Jesus is showing God's mercy toward the sinner; he is not making any change in the moral Law, (i.e., he did not suddenly make adultery OK). Jesus makes no mention of the penalty nor does he attempt to change it. Instead, recognizing the hypocrisy of the woman's accusers, Jesus challenges them by saying, "Let him who is without sin be the first to cast a stone at her" (Jn 8:7).

In this valuable lesson, Jesus teaches us that the sin of the woman's accusers is worse than hers. Jesus is calling the Pharisees to see that the pride of their hearts blinds them to their own sin, and pride is the root of all sin. The message of the Gospel is the recognition that sin and evil

have their origin in the fallen human condition. Jesus
criticizes the scribes and Pharisees for their blindness to
this truth and for their stubborn desire to merely follow
the letter of God's Law outwardly as opposed to truly
living it inwardly (as the Beatitudes teach us). Using this
same example, Jesus teaches us that the sin of adultery
has already been committed by anyone who even looks
at a woman with lust in his heart (Mt 5:28). By contrast,
Jesus calls us to be pure of heart, for doing so "is the
precondition of the vision of God" (CCC 2519).

Jesus teaches the apostles that he did not come to replace
the Law of the Old Covenant but to fulfill it (Mt 5:17; Gal
4:4-5). In the Gospel, we discover that Jesus, rather than
abolishing the Old Law, places *greater* demands upon
us by *elevating* God's Law to its ultimate perfection. For
example, in the Sermon on the Mount, Jesus tells the
disciples that true "blessedness" is found in forgiving our
enemies and praying for our persecutors (Mt 5:44). As
followers of Christ, we are called not only to follow the
law of God but to seek its highest perfection through the
power given by God's grace.

Question #33

"I've heard that Catholic bishops selected the books of the Bible. How do we know this is true?"

A. History attests to the fact that the Catholic Church, in
exercise of the authority entrusted to it by Christ himself,
ultimately discerned those books which together would
become the Bible. During the time of the early Church,
when the books of the New Testament were written, a
number of other writings existed that spoke about Jesus
and his teachings. As you can imagine, there was a great

deal of confusion as to which books were truly inspired by the Holy Spirit and which were not.

In AD 393, at the Council of Hippo, a town in northern Africa, the bishops of the Church, under the guidance and inspiration of the Holy Spirit, first determined which books would be included in the *canon* of Sacred Scripture. Later Church councils, particularly the councils of Carthage in AD 397 and 419, confirmed this decision, and the Council of Trent in 1546 formally canonized what we now recognize as the traditional books of the Bible.

The writings of the early Church Fathers confirm this process. While there are still other writings that you may hear about today (such as the *Gospel of Thomas* and the *Gospel of James*), these books were never, at any point, considered by the Church to be a part of the Bible.

Question #34

"Did the miracles mentioned in the Bible really happen?"

A. Yes, they did (see CCC 547–550). First, we need to consider the evidence in the Bible itself. For example, the Gospels offer a number of convincing arguments for the authenticity of the miracles performed by Jesus. They include: the careful recording of many of these events by eyewitnesses and by those who heard eyewitness testimony (Lk 1:1-4); the fact that the Gospel writers themselves discussed the natural doubt and disbelief that surrounded the miracles as they were happening (Mt 9:27ff, 28:17); the scrutiny of the Jewish leaders who tried to discredit them (Jn 9:13-34); and the conversions by many who initially doubted but later came to believe after what they had witnessed with their own eyes (Jn 12:9-11).

These are just a few of the many such examples in the Bible that testify to the truth of miracles.

Second, we need to remember that Jesus is alive and active in his Church today. Miracles have occurred throughout the two-thousand-year history of the Church, and they continue happening today. In fact, the normal process for canonizing a saint requires at least two miracles attributed to his or her intercessory prayer. The Church conducts thorough investigations, using reputable medical and scientific experts to make certain that the particular events have no natural explanation.

Over the years, the Church has officially recognized thousands of miracles. Many of them are well-known: the apparitions of Our Lady at Guadalupe, Lourdes, and Fatima and the numerous healings that have occurred among pilgrims to these places. Others include miracles of the Eucharist and of the Cross as well as countless others. There are a number of fine books on the subject that you can find in your local Catholic bookstore.

Question #35

"Is the biblical story of Noah and the Flood just a fable, or did it really happen?"

A. Though some modern biblical scholars have speculated that the great flood recorded in Genesis, chapters 7 and 8, is just a mythological story, the Tradition of the Church has affirmed its essential truth—namely, that God did not abandon his people but offered them an opportunity for being saved and indeed saved those who responded to his invitation (i.e., Noah and his family). In addition, the literature and oral traditions of many cultures throughout the world make reference to a great flood; some even to

Noah and the Ark. In recent years, scientists have begun to mention the strong geological evidence of a worldwide flood in ancient times. Also, since Genesis 6:14-16 gives the precise dimensions of the Ark (i.e., 450 feet long, 75 feet wide, and 45 feet high), researchers have been able to determine its exact size. One such study, conducted by John Woodmorappe and documented in his book *Noah's Ark: A Feasibility Study* (Institute for Creation Research, 1996), discovered that if you were to take the number of animals spoken of in Genesis 7 and calculate their mass and the surface area necessary to house them, the space needed fits with the exact dimensions of the ark mentioned in the Bible.

Genesis also tells us that when the flood waters subsided, Noah's Ark "came to rest on the mountains of Ararat" (Gn 8:4). Today, this region includes parts of western Armenia and eastern Turkey. The famous historian Flavius Josephus, writing in about AD 50, mentions that within this region could be found "the remains of the ark, wherein it is related that Noah escaped the deluge, and where they are still shown to us are desirous to see them."[8] Other such reports are mentioned by other notable figures, including the famous thirteenth-century Italian explorer Marco Polo. In 1295, he wrote that within this same region "there is a very tall mountain on which it is said, rests Noah's ark. This mountain is so high and wide that, it takes more than two days to walk around it. The deep snow on its peak remains year round, nobody can climb it."[9]

In recent years, there have been a number of expeditions to this remote corner of the world to look for the remains of Noah's Ark. Although many believe that the Ark may have been covered by a mud and lava flow, some of these expeditions have found artifacts at the base of Mount

Ararat that look like the remains of a very large ship. Some who visited the site also claim to have found fittings, brackets, and rivets used to secure the wooden hull of the Ark. Whether this is the actual location of what remains of Noah's Ark, we may never know for certain.

As previously mentioned, scientific analysis and historical records provide convincing evidence of the occurrence of the Flood, as well as numerous reported sightings of the remains of Noah's Ark throughout history. Such investigations are worthwhile because they help confirm what we read in Genesis. If you are interested in a further study of this topic, there are a number of resources available on the Internet, as well as books and periodicals.

Question #36

"Did Jesus really multiply the loaves and fishes? My friend's teacher said the real miracle was that the people shared their food."

A. Yes, Jesus really multiplied the loaves and fishes. The explanation of "sharing" ignores the clear, literal sense of the Gospel. It is an example of what theologians call *reductionism* (i.e., trying to explain a supernatural event in purely natural, worldly terms).

In the sixth chapter of John, the focus is entirely on Jesus' actions: It is he who shows sympathy for the people; it is he who asks the apostles about food availability; and it is he who blesses the five loaves and two fishes and orders them to be distributed among the crowd of five thousand. Before performing the miracle, St. John tells us that Jesus "knew what *he* was going to do" (Jn 6:6; emphasis added). Notice that Jesus does not ask the crowd to share. So the question to ask those who may propose the "food sharing" argument is, "Where is the evidence for that?" The text doesn't say anything about sharing. Instead, this is an idea or theory created from something other than what the Bible actually tells us.

As with all of Jesus' miracles, there is more to this one than meets the eye. In multiplying the loaves and fishes, Jesus reveals that he is the One who provides nourishment—both physically and spiritually—for his people. The majority of the sixth chapter of John is traditionally called the "Bread of Life Discourse," in which Jesus reveals that he is the living bread come down from heaven which gives life to the world (Jn 6:51, 35). The miracle of the loaves and fishes is a foreshadowing of the Eucharist. Jesus, who once miraculously fed the crowds with bread, continues to feed us today with the Bread of Life—his Body and Blood. As John tells us, "Whoever eats my flesh and drinks my blood has eternal life, and I will raise him on the last day" (Jn 6:54).

It is hard to understand why some downplay the role of Jesus in performing a miracle with the loaves and fishes. After all, if we believe in the Incarnation—God becoming man in the person of Jesus—or in the Resurrection, then why should we have a problem believing Jesus could actually multiply some loaves and fishes?

Question #37

"What's the difference between the Bibles that most Protestants use, like the King James Version, and Catholic bibles?"

A. The major difference is that most Protestant versions of the Bible—including the popular King James Version—

are missing seven books from the Old Testament. Those books are Tobit, Judith, Wisdom, Sirach, Baruch, and First and Second Maccabees. Interestingly, the original King James Version (published in 1611) included these books, but they have since been removed from most Protestant bibles or placed in a separate section called the *Apocrypha* (meaning "hidden").

In order to understand why Protestants removed these seven books, we need to go back some two centuries before the time of Christ. At that time, Jewish scholars translated the original Hebrew Old Testament into Greek. This translation became known as the *Septuagint,* and it became popular among Greek-speaking Jews and with the first Christians. In fact, the majority of the Old Testament quotations used in the New Testament are taken from the *Septuagint* translation.

Between the years AD 90 and 100, Jewish rabbis met to determine which books would be considered a part of their Bible. Many believed that these seven books, although included in the *Septuagint,* should not be included in their list of books because they were written in Greek rather than Hebrew, the original language of the other books of the Old Testament. Nevertheless, the early Christian Church accepted these books as part of the canon of Sacred Scripture. Early Church councils— at Hippo (AD 393) and Carthage (AD 397 and 419)— determined that these seven books were inspired by the Holy Spirit. This raised the number of books of the Old Testament to forty-six.

This canon of Scripture was accepted by all Christians for nearly 1,600 years. It was Martin Luther, when he translated the Bible into German in 1534, who first dropped these seven books from the list of approved books. He also called such New Testament books as Hebrews, James, Jude, and Revelation "non-canonical" based on his new, unorthodox theology. Luther's actions led to the exclusion of Tobit, Judith, Wisdom, Sirach, Baruch, and First and Second Maccabees from nearly all Protestant versions of the Bible (with the exception of the original King James Bible, as we have mentioned).

The Catholic Church has always taught that these seven Old Testament books are inspired and canonical. In reaction to Luther and the other Protestant leaders, the Council of Trent in 1546 decreed that these books be treated "with equal devotion and reverence" to the other books of the Bible. This has been reaffirmed in the *Catechism of the Catholic Church* (see CCC 120).

Question #38

"In the past, didn't the Church forbid Catholics from reading the Bible?

A. No. The Church has never forbidden Catholics from reading *approved* translations of the Bible. During the Protestant Reformation, however, the Church did ban certain *heretical* Bible translations because of the harm that the errors in these versions could do to the faith of the people.

As the *Catechism* reminds us, "The task of giving an authentic interpretation of the Word of God, whether in its written form or in the form of Tradition, has been entrusted to the living, teaching office of the Church alone" (CCC 85). It is the Church's duty to make sure that Bible translations are authentic. This is why all Catholic translations have the *Imprimatur* (approval) of a bishop.

The Church has always encouraged the reading of the Bible, the integrity of which it guards faithfully (see CCC 103). The *Catechism* affirms that "access to Sacred Scripture ought to be open wide to the Christian faithful" (CCC 131; see CCC 133).

Interestingly enough, many Protestants also had concerns over the poor quality of some sixteenth-century Bible translations. This was a main reason why the king of England commissioned the King James Version—to ensure that an accurate, reliable translation of Scripture was available to English-speaking Protestants.

Question #39

"I want to read the Bible, but I can never seem to get past Genesis. Do you have any suggestions?"

A. Actually, your experience is common. Reading the Bible is not like reading a novel. It takes effort and study because the meaning of many passages is not always obvious. This is because the Bible is not just one book but a collection of seventy-three books. These books were written over the course of about one thousand years by many authors who used a variety of literary styles— history, poetry, prophecy, etc.—to teach the truth God revealed to them. Why should we expect that a "book" written in ancient times in foreign cultures would be easy to understand? We need to read the Bible "in light of the same Spirit by whom it was written" (CCC 111) and within "the living Tradition of the whole Church" (CCC 113).

Each week at Sunday Mass, we hear four readings proclaimed: one from the Old Testament (the First Reading), a part of the book of Psalms (the Responsorial Psalm), one from the New Testament (the Second Reading), and one from Matthew, Mark, Luke, or John (the Gospel Reading). If you are getting stuck at Genesis, why not try reading something from these other parts of the Bible?

To gain strength or find spiritual guidance, you may want to read and reflect on some of the practical books of advice in the Old Testament, like Proverbs, Wisdom, or Sirach. The New Testament is the story of the early Church, and much of it is actually very interesting and pretty easy to follow. For example, the Acts of the Apostles records what happened after Jesus ascended into heaven. There are some awesome stories and miracles in this book, like people getting captured, angels breaking people out of jail, people possessed by demons being healed, shipwrecks, (and the list goes on)! Finally, reading the words of Jesus and the stories about him in the Gospels will always provide you with plenty to think and pray about as you continue to grow in your faith.

While your desire to read the Bible starting with Genesis is a wonderful goal, it's probably not the best approach. Here's a suggestion: Begin your study of the Bible by reading those books that tell the "story" of salvation. There is an excellent Bible study program called *The Great Adventure Bible Timeline* (published by Ascension Press). This program helps you focus on the fourteen "narrative" books of the Bible that tell this story and teaches you how the people, places, and events are linked together. *The Great Adventure* also shows you how the remaining fifty-nine books of the Bible fit into the story. For more information, go to AscensionPress.com.

Chapter 4

JESUS CHRIST

Question #40

"How can Jesus be a man and God at the same time?"

A. Next to the Trinity, this is the most profound mystery of our faith. But remember: In theological terms, a "mystery" is not something we can know *nothing* about. Rather, a mystery is a truth so profound that we cannot know *everything* about it; our limited human intellects cannot understand it fully. Since the Incarnation touches on the very nature of God—who is infinite—we should not be surprised that we, as finite creatures, have a little trouble grasping this reality.

In the Bible, the opening words of John's Gospel affirm Jesus' divinity, calling him *the Word*: "In the beginning was the Word, and the Word was with God, and the Word was God. He was in the beginning with God; all things were made through him, and without him was not anything made that was made." (Jn 1:1-3). By calling him "the Word," St. John affirms that Jesus is the fullness of God's revelation who came into the world as a man for our salvation.

Of course, it is no coincidence that the words, "In the beginning," are the first words of the Old Testament as well. In Genesis 1:1, they refer to God's Creation of the world. St. John uses them to affirm the pre-existence of Jesus as God, through whom the world was created. In the New Testament, St. Paul encourages the Christians of Philippi with a clear statement of Jesus' divinity: "Though he was in the form of God, [Jesus] did not count equality with God a thing to be grasped, but emptied himself, taking the form of a servant, being born in the likeness of men" (Phil 2:6-7).

While Jesus' conception two thousand years ago in the womb of his mother, Mary, marked the beginning of his existence as a human being, he actually existed from all eternity as the Second Person of the Trinity. As St. John writes, "And the Word became flesh and dwelt among us, full of grace and truth; we have beheld his glory, glory as of the only Son from the Father" (Jn 1:14).

According to Church dogma, Jesus has two *natures,* human and divine, which tell us *what* he is—the God-man. These two natures are joined in the one divine *person* of Jesus—which tells us *who* he is—the Second Person of the Trinity. This mystery is called the *hypostatic union.* So Jesus is inseparably true God and true man (CCC 469, 470, 473, 477, 481, 482).

Just like you and me, Jesus has a human will, a human soul, a human intellect, and a human body. But he also possesses a divine nature which was evident during his public ministry in many ways: in his miracles, his knowledge of the future, his power over nature, his authority over demons, his ability to know human thoughts, and his forgiveness of sins. Most profoundly, Jesus' divinity is seen in his resurrection from the dead and his ascension into heaven.

Question #41

"Doesn't the Trinity mean there are three Persons in Jesus?"

A. No. It sounds like you've confused the Trinity—three Persons in one God—with the two natures of Jesus. As the Son of God, Jesus is the Second Person of the Holy Trinity. So Jesus is one divine Person with two natures, human and divine.

In the Trinity, each of the divine Persons is really distinct from the other two. Each is fully God—meaning, the Father is not the Son nor is he the Holy Spirit. Likewise, the Holy Spirit is not the Son. However, because they are united in the one Godhead, they possess the same divine *nature*. Therefore, as the Council of Florence teaches, it is entirely proper to say that "because of that unity, the Father is wholly in the Son and wholly in the Holy Spirit; the Son is wholly in the Father and wholly in the Holy Spirit; the Holy Spirit is wholly in the Father and wholly in the Son" (CCC 255).

At the Council of Nicea (AD 325), the Church declared that Jesus is *homoousious* with the Father. Don't worry—you can be sure that this word won't show up on your SAT or ACT score. But *homoousious* is a valuable Greek term used to show that Jesus is "one in being" with the Father (or "of the same essence" as the Father). Jesus himself taught this when he said, "He who sent me is with me" (Jn 8:29), and, "I am in the Father and the Father in me" (Jn 14:11). In this sense, we know that wherever Jesus is, the Father and the Holy Spirit are there as well, but they remain three distinct Persons within the one Holy Trinity.

Question #42

"In the Creed every Sunday, we say that Jesus was 'begotten, not made.' What's the difference?"

A. The Creed uses the expression "begotten" to emphasize that there never was a time when Jesus, the Second Person of the Trinity, did not exist. If the Son had been "made," he would have had a beginning at some point in time. As a result, he would not be God. "Begotten" means that the Son exists because of the Father and *proceeds* (comes) from him. The Son has been proceeding from the Father for all eternity.

Here's an analogy: Imagine an eternally existing sun, one that never had a beginning but simply *was.* Such a sun would have been generating light from all eternity. So, you may ask, when did the sun begin generating light? At no point in time, since it was always coming from the eternally existing sun. This is a way we can understand how Jesus is "begotten" by the Father—he has been proceeding from him for all eternity.

Question #43

"If Jesus was God, why did he say that some things were only known to the Father, like when the end of the world would happen?"

A. As we discussed in a previous answer, Jesus is a divine Person who possesses both a divine and a human nature. This has been the constant teaching of the Church from the very beginning. So Jesus is fully human, like us in every way—except sin. When the Son of God became man, he took on a true human soul, endowed with human intellect and knowledge. By its nature, human knowledge is limited.

However, because Jesus is a divine Person, he "enjoyed in his human knowledge the fullness of understanding of the eternal plans he had come to reveal" (CCC 474). In other words, as the Son of God, Jesus was always united to his Father in heaven—"I am in the Father and the Father is in me" (Jn 14:11). Throughout his earthly life, Jesus' knowledge reveals his divinity: he demonstrates foreknowledge of the events surrounding his passion, death, and resurrection; he discusses the future destruction of Jerusalem; he tells the apostles what events will occur at the end times; and he demonstrates his ability to know the secret thoughts of human hearts.

As to when the end of the world would occur, Jesus does say, "But of that day or that hour no one knows, not even the angels in heaven, nor the Son, but only the Father" (Mk 13:32). But this does not imply that he is ignorant on the subject. In the Acts of the Apostles, Jesus tells his disciples, "It is not for you to know times or seasons which the Father has fixed by his own authority" (Acts 1:7). In other words, the disclosure of such information was not part of his mission of salvation; he simply was not sent to reveal it (see CCC 474).

Question #44

"What makes Jesus different from other famous religious leaders like Mohammad, Buddha, or Confucius?"

A. To begin with, only Jesus claimed to be both human and *divine*. Furthermore, Jesus proved his divinity through his many miracles, especially through his resurrection from the dead and ascension into heaven. Mohammad, Buddha, and Confucius may have been prominent religious leaders, but each of them ultimately died—and no one ever claimed to have seen them walking among the living after their deaths, as hundreds witnessed Jesus doing after his death and resurrection (see 1 Cor 15:4-8; Acts 1:22).

Also, only Jesus claimed a divine pre-existence prior to his birth as a human being. You may remember the scene in the Gospel in which Jesus, speaking to the scribes and Pharisees, says, "Abraham your father rejoiced to see my day; he saw it and was glad ... Before Abraham came to be, I AM" (Jn 8:56). In this passage and others and throughout the four Gospels, Jesus' divinity is shown. Not only did he exist before the world began, but he also demonstrated his power over the world, causing people to say, "What sort of man is this, whom even the winds and the sea obey?" (Mt 8:27). No one else demonstrated such marvelous signs and wonders, such that even the most hard-hearted came to believe in him (Jn 11:45).

Among the religious leaders you mention, only Jesus' life was prophesied before his birth. In the book of Isaiah, for example, we read that the Messiah would "heal" and "save" and "perform miracles" (see Is 35:4-6), including making "the deaf hear, the blind see" (Is 29:18). In the Psalms, we see that the Messiah will "pray for his enemies" (Ps 109:4); speak in parables (see Ps 78:2); and be rejected by his own people (see Ps 118:22-23). In all, there are more than a hundred prophecies in the Old Testament that foretold Jesus' coming as the Messiah.

The *entire* Old Testament is a preparation for the coming of Jesus, the Messiah who was promised by God to redeem the world and bring salvation to mankind. Ultimately, this is what separates Jesus from anyone else. Only Jesus is the Son of God, sent by the Father to die for our sins, who conquers sin and death through his passion, death, and resurrection. Furthermore, he establishes his Church on earth and through it provides all mankind the means to eternal life.

Question #45

"My Jehovah's Witness friend says that Jesus is actually the archangel Michael. I know this is wrong, but how can I respond to him?"

A. Jehovah's Witnesses (officially known as the Watchtower Bible and Tract Society of New York), a religious sect founded in the late nineteenth century by former atheist Charles Taze Russell, do not believe in the Trinity. They teach that only God the Father is truly God, and they call him *Jehovah*. Jesus, they claim, is not divine—he was created by Jehovah and is actually the archangel Michael. Jesus, in their view, is the first and highest of all created beings, and is actually the Creator of the world.

In explaining the first coming of Christ, Jehovah's Witnesses explain that Michael gave up his existence as an angel by allowing God to transfer his "spirit" to earth, thus becoming a man, Jesus Christ. They also claim that although Jesus was crucified (not on a cross but rather on an upright stake) and rose from the dead, only his *spirit*—not his body—was resurrected. When his spirit ascended into heaven, Jesus reclaimed his existence as the archangel Michael.

To respond to your friend, here are a couple of things you want to consider. First, you should charitably point out to him that Jehovah's Witnesses beliefs about Jesus are contrary not only to the teachings of the Catholic Church but also to those of the Eastern Orthodox and Protestant churches as well. In other words, *no other Christians* believe—or have ever believed—such radical ideas.

Secondly, Jehovah's Witnesses are very well-practiced in explaining what they believe. They are skilled at using selected verses from the Bible—no matter how badly they are misinterpreted—to defend their arguments. (You may want to point out that the New World Bible, the official translation of the Watchtower Society, purposely mistranslates the original Greek of the New Testament to support Witnesses theology.)

In other words, you need to be equally prepared to present Catholic truth by studying the Bible and the *Catechism* (see CCC 422–682). In addition, there are a number of valuable resources you can use, including Jason Evert's *Answering Jehovah's Witnesses,* and the following tracts by Catholic Answers (catholic.com): *Stumpers for Jehovah's Witnesses* and *More Stumpers for Jehovah's Witnesses.*

Above all else, pray and allow God's grace to work through you in bringing the truth to your friend. Try to avoid getting into a heated argument with him, remembering the words of St. Peter to always explain ourselves "with gentleness and reverence" (1 Pt 3:16).

Question #46

"If Jesus was Jewish, why are we Catholic?"

A. Remember: Christianity has its roots in Judaism. Within God's plan of salvation for mankind, the Savior was to be born of the Jewish people, from the "stump of Jesse" and "the house of David" (Is 11:1; Lk 1:32). The entire Old Testament is the story of how God prepares the

Chosen People of Israel for the coming of the *Messiah* (or "Anointed One") of God who would free all people, Jew and Gentile alike, from sin.

However, when Jesus came, many of the Jewish people did not recognize him as the Messiah who had been promised them. Many of them believed the Messiah would be a military or political leader, like King David, who would defeat the enemies of the Jewish nation and raise it up again to its previous earthly glory. When these expectations were not met by Jesus, many rejected him. However, some did believe in him. In fact, the majority of the early Christians were Jews: all of the twelve apostles, for example.

The most important reason that we are Catholic is because Jesus founded the Catholic Church and promised that he would always be with it (Mt 28:20). Jesus put Peter and the apostles in charge of caring for and guiding his Church when he ascended into heaven. Later, at Pentecost, Jesus sent the Holy Spirit to set the Church alive with power (Acts 2:1-43). It is important to remember that the Jews were waiting for someone who would reunite the twelve tribes of Israel. In fact, religious Jews of today still believe the Messiah will come and accomplish this. Unfortunately, most of them do not believe that Jesus was the Messiah, and they don't recognize that he actually did reunite the twelve tribes of Israel when he founded the Church on the twelve apostles.

As Christians, we should always appreciate the special relationship that exists between the Church and the Jewish people. As the *Catechism* reminds us, "When she delves into her own mystery, the Church, the People of God in the New Covenant, discovers her link with the

Jewish people, the first to hear the Word of God" (CCC 839). In effect, then we can say that all Christians are "spiritually Jewish" because our faith is the fulfillment of the promises God made to his Chosen People.

Question #47

"Why did people hate Jesus and want him killed? What did he do to them?"

A. When Jesus was presented in the Temple as an infant, the prophet Simeon proclaimed that he would be "a sign that will be contradicted" (Lk 2:34). Throughout his public ministry, Jesus was continually tested by the scribes and Pharisees who were seeking to find fault with him. Why? Because he challenged them to set a better example for the people. He challenged them to do more than teach God's Law; he called them to *live* God's Law and to repent of their hypocrisy. Due to human pride and the hardness of their hearts, they hated Jesus and conspired to find an opportunity to do away with him.

Actually, Jesus was threatened with death throughout his public ministry. One such incident occurred when he returned his hometown—Nazareth—and preached in its synagogue. The Gospel tells us that the people "rose up, drove him out of town, and led him to the brow of the hill on which their town had been built, to hurl him down headlong. But he passed through the midst of them and went away" (Lk 4:29-30). The people had taken offense that the same Jesus whom they had known since he was a child ("Isn't this the son of Joseph?"—Lk 4:22) was suddenly declaring himself to be a prophet and comparing himself to the prophet Elijah. For many, this was too much; it was considered blasphemous. Others were perhaps resentful of Jesus and found his sudden celebrity difficult to accept.

There are other reasons why people wanted Jesus dead. The majority of the Sanhedrin—the chief Jewish council— were fearful of Jesus' popularity because "all will believe in him, and the Romans will come and take away both our land and our nation" (Jn 11:48). Caiaphas, the high priest, responded to this concern by stating, "You know nothing, nor do you consider that it is better for you that one man should die instead of the people, so that the whole nation may not perish" (Jn 11:49-50). From then on, they began plotting to have Jesus killed.

Question #48
"Why is Jesus' death so important?"

A. The *Catechism* teaches us that Jesus' suffering and death on the Cross accomplished two things: "the definitive redemption of men" and the restoration of "man to communion with God through the blood of the covenant, which was poured out for many for the forgiveness of sins" (CCC 613; see Jn 1:29; Mt 26:28). In other words, Jesus offered his life for us in order to make reparation for the sins—past, present, and future—of the whole world. As the *Catechism* goes on to explain, "Jesus atoned for our faults and made satisfaction for our sins to the Father" (CCC 615). Through his death on the Cross, Jesus makes right again our relationship with the Father and allows us to have a share once more in his blessed and eternal life.

Because our relationship with God was cut off by original sin, only God is capable of bringing man back into communion with him. By himself, man cannot find the path that is necessary to lead him back to God. Also, because of God's infinite greatness, no reparation for sin as accomplished by man alone could ever satisfy the debt that is owed God. An infinite debt logically calls for an infinite response. In order to restore our friendship with him, only God himself can satisfy the debt of human sin. Jesus' death on the Cross pays that debt. By inviting each of us to take up our cross and follow him. He asks each one of us to participate directly in his redemptive work through the sacrificial offering of our own lives. "Christ also suffered for [us], leaving [us] an example so that [we] should follow in his steps" (Mt 16:24; 1 Pt 2:21; CCC 618).

Question #49

"Is the Shroud of Turin really the burial cloth of Jesus?"

A. First, here is some background information on the Shroud of Turin. The Shroud is currently stored in a secure, climate-controlled vault in the cathedral church of Turin (Torino), Italy, and is only displayed occasionally. It has been in Turin since 1578 and has a documented history dating back to the year 500, when there are historical records of it having been venerated in Jerusalem.

In recent years, there has been much scientific examination and analysis conducted on the Shroud. In 1898, an amazing discovery was made by a man by the name of Secundo Pia. After photographing the Shroud and developing the film, he discovered that the black and white negative of the image in the photograph clearly shows the figure of a man in much greater detail. This sparked considerable interest in further study of the Shroud.

In 1978, the Shroud of Turin Research Project, consisting of a group of respected scientists from around the world, was formed to conduct extensive research on the Shroud. Among other discoveries resulting from this research, it was determined that the image on the Shroud was indeed that of a man who had suffered the brutal death of crucifixion. The wounds in the hands, the feet, and the side of the man in the image correspond to the wounds suffered by Jesus as mentioned in the Gospel. Furthermore, blood stains found throughout head area as well as across the back and shoulder areas correspond well with the accounts mentioned in the Gospel—the crowning of thorns upon Jesus' head and the scourging (i.e., whipping) he endured prior to his crucifixion. The blood itself was discovered to be human blood of the type AB group. At the conclusion of their work, the scientists of the project were convinced that the Shroud could not have been the work of an artist or a forgery. Without actually declaring the Shroud to be the historic burial cloth of Jesus, they simply concluded that the image on the Shroud remains an ongoing mystery requiring further investigation and chemical study.

More recent study of the Shroud has involved carbon dating testing, which was conducted in 1988. Although the results of this dating seemed to shed doubt on whether the Shroud is old enough to have been around at the time of Jesus two thousand years ago, many scientists believe the results were flawed because they failed to factor in such considerations as the presence of contaminants, which may have altered the findings. In addition, testing was actually done on a portion of the Shroud that was sewn in later.

In all, there is a lot of evidence that seems to support the Shroud's authenticity as the burial cloth of Jesus.[10] But it is important to remember that belief in the Shroud as Jesus' actual burial cloth is *not* a matter of faith. In other words, we are free to believe or disbelieve its authenticity. However, St. John Paul II and other recent popes have certainly recognized the Shroud as a relic worthy of our veneration because it is such a powerful reminder of what our Lord Jesus suffered for our salvation.

Question #50
"How old was Jesus when he died on the Cross?"

A. Traditionally, the age attributed to Jesus at the time of his death is thirty-three. We know that Luke's Gospel states that Jesus was "about thirty years of age when he began his ministry" (Lk 3:23). All four Gospel writers—Matthew, Mark, Luke, and John—indicate that the public ministry of Jesus began with his baptism in the river Jordan by John the Baptist.

From this starting point, the Gospel of John indicates that Jesus' public ministry spanned the commemoration of three Jewish Passovers, a period of at least three years. From this fact, we can deduce that Jesus would have been about thirty-three years old at the time of his crucifixion. This figure has been widely accepted throughout the two-thousand-year history of Christianity.

Question #51
"Did Jesus have a last name?"

A. This is actually a very interesting question. When we refer to Jesus as "Christ," we are simply affirming that Jesus is *the Christ*, or Messiah. (*Christos* is the Greek form of the Hebrew *Messiah*, meaning "anointed one.")

Use of family (or "last") names is a relatively new phenomenon, dating back only four hundred or five hundred years. Up to that time, people lived in small towns or in rural areas and generally went by first names only. This was the case in Jesus' time. Often, a person's town name was added to clarify who was being spoken about (e.g., Jesus of Nazareth, Joseph of Arimathea, Simon the Cyrenean).

Modern names such as "Johnson" and "Jackson" developed from someone actually being the son of someone named "John" or "Jack." Names such as "Carpenter," "Baker," and "Smith" are examples of a person's occupation being used as family names. In the Gospel, the name of one of the apostles, Bartholomew, simply means "son of Tolmai" (*Bar* meaning "son" in Aramaic). Jesus, when referring to Simon Peter, asks him, "Simon, Son of John, do you love me?" (Jn 21:16). Here, he identifies Simon Peter as the son of his father, John (or Jona).

Throughout the Gospel, Jesus is referred to as "Jesus of Nazareth" (Mk 16:6), "Jesus of Nazareth" (Jn 18:7), "Jesus, son of David" (Mt 9:27), "Jesus, the carpenter's son" (Mt 13:55), and "Jesus, the son of Joseph" (Jn 6:42). By today's standards, any of these could have been used as the equivalent of Jesus' "last name."

Question #52

"The Bible indicates that when anyone touched Jesus, he or she was cured. If this is true, why aren't people cured when they receive the Eucharist?"

A. When we read the Gospel, it is clear that not everyone who came into contact with Jesus experienced an immediate and identifiable cure. The Gospel relays to us the story of the woman who was suffering from a prolonged hemorrhage of which doctors could find no cure. Upon seeing Jesus pass by, she reached out in faith and was convinced that she need only touch Jesus' cloak to be cured. Upon doing so, Jesus, "aware at once that power had gone out from him, turned around in the crowd and asked, 'Who touched my clothes?'" His disciples immediately pointed out to him that many people had been "pressing upon" him. Upon finding the woman, Jesus said to her, "Daughter, your faith has saved you. Go in peace and be cured of your affliction." Jesus knew that because of the strength of the woman's faith, her touching him had an entirely different effect upon her than it did for anyone else who might have touched him (Mk 5:21-34; see Mt 9:19-22, Lk 8:43-48).

Furthermore, the *Catechism* reminds us that "communion with the Body and Blood of Christ increases the communicant's union with the Lord, forgives his venial sins, and preserves him from grave sin" (CCC 1416). Throughout the two-thousand-year history of the Church, there have been countless miracles and cures directly attributed to the Holy Eucharist. Some of the more celebrated ones are discussed in the book *This Is My Body, This Is My Blood (Volumes I and II)* by Bob and Penny Lord. This inspiring book can be found in Catholic bookstores or on the Internet.

Chapter 5

THE CATHOLIC FAITH
AND THE CHURCH

Question #53

"How do we know that the Catholic Church is the one that Jesus founded?"

A. One way we can know this is simply by looking at history. The Catholic Church is the only church that can trace its origin directly and uninterruptedly back to Jesus. All other Christian denominations were founded by men at distinct points in history—e.g., the Lutheran church was founded by Martin Luther in 1517, the Anglican church by King Henry VIII in 1534, and the Reformed church by John Calvin in 1536. Only the Catholic Church has an uninterrupted line of bishops that stretches back directly to the apostles.

In addition to the historical record, we can also look at some essential aspects that the Church founded by Christ should have—traditionally known as the four "marks" of the Church. We affirm these marks each time we say the Creed at Mass.

Briefly, the true Church of Christ must be:

1. *One*—this means that the Church is unique (i.e., there is only one Church founded by Jesus) and united in

one faith. In the Gospel of John, Jesus prayed that the apostles would be "one"—united—just as he and the Father are "one" (Jn 10:30). Division and dissension in the Church are always contrary to the will of Jesus, but both frequently occur as the result of our sinful nature (see CCC 814). It is the responsibility of all Christians, but especially the pope and bishops, to promote unity among the followers of Christ (see CCC 879).

2. *Holy*—simply speaking, the Church is holy because its founder, Jesus, is holy. As a result, we can say that the Church is holy in its beliefs, worship, sacraments, government, and members (especially in the saints). In spite of human weakness, the Church's holiness flows from the very holiness of God himself.

3. *Catholic*—from the Greek word meaning "universal," the Church's faith extends to the entire world. The Church is not limited to one language, race, culture, or nation—it is intended for everyone, of every place and time.

4. *Apostolic*—before his ascension, Jesus told his apostles to "go, and make disciples of all nations ... And behold I am with you always, until the end of the age" (Mt 28:19-20). With these words, Jesus gave the apostles "the great commission" to preach the gospel to the whole world, a mission that will continue until the end of time. To accomplish this mission, the apostles needed to appoint successors so that their work would continue after their deaths. As the book of Acts tells us: "... they designated such men and then made the ruling that likewise on their death other proven men should take over the ministry" (CCC 861; see also CCC 860 and Acts 20:28). In the original Greek of the

New Testament, these men were known as *episkopoi* (meaning "overseers") from which we get the English word "bishop." Today's bishops are descendants of the apostles; they are our modern-day apostles.

These four marks—*one, holy, catholic,* and *apostolic*—are found only in the Catholic Church. Although many elements of truth are found outside the Church in other faiths, "in [the Catholic Church] subsists the fullness of the means of salvation which [Jesus himself] has willed" (CCC 830).

Question #54

"Why do we call it the *Catholic* Church? Where did this name come from?"

A. The word "catholic" comes from the Greek word *katholikos,* meaning "universal." This means that the Church and its teachings are intended for all people and all times. The word was first used by St. Ignatius of Antioch (AD 35–107) in his letter to the Christians of Smyrna: "Where there is Christ Jesus, there is the catholic church."[11]

For the first one thousand years of Christianity, all Christians were united and identified themselves as members of the "Catholic" Church. During this period, believing Christians followed the leadership of the pope and the bishops in communion with him. Then, in AD 1054, a *schism* ("separation" or "split") occurred between the Western and Eastern churches. This split happened more for cultural and political reasons than over theological issues. Today, these separated churches are collectively known as the Eastern Orthodox, of which there are many "national" churches (e.g., Russian Orthodox, Greek Orthodox, Romanian Orthodox, etc.).

Although the Orthodox have valid bishops and accept most Catholic beliefs (e.g., the apostolic succession of bishops, the real presence of Jesus in the Eucharist, the seven sacraments, devotion to Mary, etc.), they do not recognize the full authority of the pope and some later dogmatic teachings. Nearly five hundred years later, a second (and even more damaging) split occurred within the Church—the Protestant Reformation—which gave rise to the thousands of Christian denominations we see today.

In spite of these divisions, Jesus wants his Church to be united. He prayed to the Father that his followers "may be one, even as we are one" (Jn 17:22). The *Catechism* reminds us that Jesus gave unity to the Church from the beginning: "This unity ... subsists in the Catholic Church as something she can never lose, and we hope that it will continue to increase until the end of time" (CCC 820).

Question #55

"Is the Church really necessary? Doesn't it really come down to your personal relationship with Jesus?"

A. In the end, it *does* come down to our relationship with Jesus. But we are not saved on our own. We need the community Jesus himself established to be the source of his grace in our lives—the Church (see CCC 781). It is in the Church that our faith is born, nourished, and strengthened through the sacraments, especially by the Holy Eucharist.

The *Catechism* reminds us that faith is necessary for salvation. Faith is a supernatural gift from God, and in order to believe, man requires the interior assistance of the Holy Spirit as given to him in baptism (see CCC 183, 179).

Though faith involves a personal act—belief in God and his Son, Jesus—it is not an *isolated* act. "You have not given yourself faith as you have not given yourself life. The believer has received faith from others ..." (CCC 166). It is the Church, therefore, that is the instrument through which we come to know and believe in Jesus (see CCC 168). As St. Cyprian, a great third-century Church father, teaches: "No one can have God as Father who does not have the Church as Mother" (CCC 181).[12]

The *Catechism* eloquently states that the Church exists as "a plan born in the Father's heart" (CCC 759). We have been called by God to be a part of the Church. Sent to fulfill his Father's will, Jesus formed his Church as a community with the twelve apostles and Peter as their head: "The Twelve and the other disciples share in Christ's mission and his power," for the purpose of building up of the kingdom of God on earth, which is the Church" (CCC 765; see also 763). We see this building of the kingdom when Jesus sent them out two by two and gave them authority over unclean spirits (see Mk 6:7). Shortly before his ascension into heaven, Jesus commissioned his apostles to "go, therefore, and make disciples of all nations, baptizing them ... teaching them to observe all that I have commanded you" (Mt 28:19-20).

Question #56

"My friend thinks it's wrong to say that one Christian can have authority over another Christian. How do we know that Jesus gave the Church authority?"

A. The belief that no Christian can have authority over another is common among evangelical and fundamentalist Protestants. It is rooted in the notion that the Bible is the ultimate authority in all matters. But, curiously enough, the Bible itself does not support such a position.

Both the Old and New Testaments provide numerous examples of how God gives certain individuals the authority to rule over his people. In Deuteronomy, the people of Israel are placed under the authority of the judges and priests (Dt 17:1-13). In the Gospel of Matthew, Jesus gives authority to His Church and decrees that whoever does not listen to the judgment of its leaders brings judgment upon himself and should be treated as an outsider by the community (Mt 18:15-20).

In addition, Jesus confers authority over his Church to the apostle Peter by saying, "I will give you the keys of the kingdom of heaven, and whatever you bind on earth shall be bound in heaven, and whatever you loose on earth shall be loosed in heaven" (Mt 16:19). The power of *binding* and *loosing* was understood by the Jews to be the power of permitting and forbidding. This same authority has been handed down to all of Peter's successors of the past two thousand years, right up to the present pope.

In the Old Testament, Moses handed on his authority to Joshua by laying his hands on him (Dt 34:9). The authority of the apostles is passed on to their successors in the same manner (1 Tm 4:14; 2 Tm 1:6). Exhorting and reproving with this authority (Ti 2:15), the bishops guide the Church, and Christians are required to listen to them: "Do not be led away by diverse and strange teachings … Obey your leaders and submit to them; for they are keeping watch over your souls" (Heb 13:9, 17).

The authority of the Church comes directly from Jesus, who gives the Church this role of shepherding the faithful. By exercising this power, the Church makes Christ's voice present in the world throughout history. As Jesus tells his apostles, "Whoever hears you, hears me, and whoever rejects you, rejects me" (Lk 10:16). If we want to have a true relationship with Jesus, we must always strive to "hear" the teachings of his Church.

Question #57

"If God gave us free will to make our own choices, then why do I have to listen to the Church?"

A. You are absolutely correct that God has given us free will to make our own choices. If he didn't, we would not be human beings made in his image and likeness; we would be robots. But true freedom does not mean doing whatever we want. True freedom means having the ability to do what we *ought* to do—in other words, to do what is right and what is ultimately best for us and others. Because of our human weakness, we do not always use our freedom properly. We sometimes make wrong choices, and sometimes we make these errors out of ignorance.

Fortunately, our heavenly Father is fully aware of our needs; he knows exactly what is best for us. Through Jesus, he invites us to follow the path that leads to him. Why? Because he has created us for himself so that we may know, love, and serve him in this life and be happy with him for all eternity when our earthly lives are over. Through the exercise of our free will, we can choose either to accept or reject God's invitation.

Because God respects our free will, he never forces us to do good or to choose him. Instead, he grants us certain graces to help us respond to his invitation. We receive these graces most abundantly and effectively through our participation in the sacraments (baptism, penance, confirmation, holy eucharist, holy matrimony, holy orders, and the anointing of the sick), which can only be administered to us through the Church.

As discussed in the previous answer, the Gospel clearly states that when we listen to the teaching office of the Church—as represented by the pope and the bishops united with him—we are listening to the voice of Jesus (Lk 10:16). In other words, if we truly seek to follow Jesus, we must follow the teachings of his Church.

Question #58

Why should I be Catholic when there are so many hypocrites in the Church?

A. Here's a way to look at this question: Imagine you lived in Palestine in Old Testament times. You would have seen many Israelites—God's Chosen People—committing terrible sins (e.g., David's adultery and the murder of Uriah; see 2 Sam 11:1-27). If you judged the truth of their religion based on the behavior of its believers, you would run the risk of overlooking the great truths and wonders that God revealed to them. Similarly, if you had lived in the time of Jesus, you would have seen him repeatedly rebuke the scribes and Pharisees as "hypocrites." But you would also have seen Jesus remind the people that the scribes and Pharisees held legitimate authority: "The scribes and the Pharisees sit on Moses' seat; so practice and observe whatever they tell you, but not what they do; for they preach, but do not practice" (Mt 23:2-3).

Ideally, it would have been better for the scribes and Pharisees to have "practiced what they preached." But not all them were evil men. Many of them actually believed—

or came to believe—in Jesus. Even among the apostles, we know that Judas betrayed Jesus for thirty pieces of silver. But the others went to their deaths or were imprisoned for their commitment to the faith.

To judge the truth of the Catholic Faith on the basis of the sinful actions of some of its members is like judging the quality of a Ferrari or Porsche by the quality of its driver. A driver who drives recklessly and crashes the car does not make the car bad. It is the bad driver that's the problem. In this analogy, we are all responsible in some way to seeing that the car is driven properly. In order to get a true picture of the sanctifying grace and power of the Church, we can look to the examples set by the great saints. They embraced the means of holiness given to the Church by Jesus (i.e., the Bible, the Liturgy, and the sacraments) and reached great holiness.

Every human being on the planet is a sinner, but all are called to be saints. In this way, it is true that we are all hypocrites to *some* degree. This is precisely the reason why Jesus came among us as a man, so that through his death and resurrection, we all may be freed from the bondage of sin and death and become holy. The Church has continued the work of winning souls to Christ for two thousand years. In the Gospel, Jesus himself is criticized for associating with sinners and tax collectors. Jesus responded by saying, "Those who are well do not need a physician, but the sick do. I did not come to call the righteous but sinners" (Mk 2:17).

Remember: Jesus did not ask Peter if Phillip loved him, or if James loved him, or even if his brother, Andrew, loved him. He asked Peter, "Do *you* love me?" (Jn 21:17; emphasis added).

Jesus cares more about the answer we give him about our own faith—and our own love—for him than he does about the hypocrisy in the lives of others.

Question #59

"My non-Catholic friend says that the Church is guilty of torturing and killing thousands of people during the Inquisition. Is this true?"

A. Your friend's statement has to be considered in light of history. First, let's look at exactly what the Inquisition was and how it worked.

The Inquisition acted as a *tribunal* (or court) in which Church officials, appointed by the pope, judged the cases of those accused of *heresy* (i.e., false beliefs). One of the primary concerns of the Inquisition was to ensure that justice was done and that false charges were dismissed. You need to remember that during this period in history, the Catholic Church was the *only* Christian church in Western Europe. There was no separation of Church and state; the Church and civil governments worked together in opposing heresy because it was also viewed as treason against the state. When someone was found guilty of heresy, it was the civil authority—not the Church—that enforced the penalty.

The Inquisition began in the twelfth century in response to the growing popularity of the Albigensian heresy. Since this movement taught, among other things, that the body was evil and that marriage and children were a curse to be avoided, the Albigensians were a threat not only to the faith but also to common good of society as a whole.

Of those found guilty of heresy, only a small number were actually condemned to death. Most faced the usual punishment of imprisonment. Unfortunately, it is true that civil authorities did occasionally use torture in order to gain a confession. We need to understand that during this time in history, civil rulers often used torture as a means of punishment. It was the pope, in fact, who spoke out against using torture, and this led to it being used less frequently.

In the fifteenth century, the Inquisition was established in Spain. Unfortunately, its activities were largely under the control of the Spanish monarchy, and this led to a number of abuses. While we should not try to "whitewash" or excuse these abuses, at the same time, we should not forget the important role the Inquisition played in preserving the integrity of the Faith and in preventing anarchy in a number of countries. Also, the Catholic Church was not alone in using such practices. During the Protestant Reformation, torture and death were widely used against Catholics and other "heretics." In all fairness, we need to view these events in their proper historical context and not judge them by today's standards.

The modern media, some history textbooks, and other recent works like *The Da Vinci Code* try to paint a picture of the Church as slaughtering hundreds of thousands, even millions, of people. In reality, the most liberal of solid historical estimates is that there may have been five thousand such executions over the course of roughly three hundred years. It is true that wrongfully killing even one person is a tragedy, but the truth about the Inquisition is much different from what some people try to make it out to be.

Here are some recommended books on the subject: *Inquisition* by Edward Peters (University of California

Press, 1989) and *Characters of the Inquisition* by William Thomas Walsh (TAN Books, 1987).

Question #60

"I've seen articles in the media about how the Church didn't do anything for the Jews during World War II. Is this true?"

A. The articles and reports you are referring to are part of one of the most outrageous media fabrications in modern history. As nearly every reputable historian will attest, the suggestion that the Catholic Church did nothing to help Jews escape Nazi oppression during World War II is totally false. This claim is nothing more than popular anti-Catholic propaganda of the worst kind.

Here are the facts: In 1937, Pope Pius XI, responding to the rise of Adolf Hitler's oppression of Jews, condemned Nazism in his encyclical letter *Mit Brennender Sorge*, "With Burning Sorrow." (Interestingly, this encyclical was written in German—not the traditional Latin—so that its message would be clearly understood by the Nazis.) His successor, Pius XII, took office in 1939 just as World War II was beginning.

By 1940, Nazi Germany had conquered most of Europe and Northern Africa and had allied itself with Italy, which was then led by the dictator Benito Mussolini. As a result, the Vatican, located in the heart of the Italian capital of Rome, found itself isolated and cut off from the rest of the world. However, this did not deter the pope from continuing to speak out against the actions of the Nazis. For example, in his Christmas message of 1941, Pius XII specifically denounced the persecution of the Jewish people, something that many people were denying was occurring. The *New York Times* praised his message and wrote, "This Christmas more than ever Pope Pius XII is a lonely voice crying out in the silence of a continent ... When he assails violent occupation of territory, the exile and persecution of human beings for no reason other than race or political opinion ... the 'impartial' judgment is like a verdict in our high court of justice."[13] In other words, the editors of the *New York Times* at that time affirmed that the pope was speaking out against Nazi oppression of the Jews.

In addition to official Church statements, the Vatican issued numerous protests directly to Hitler's government. This fact was attested during the Nuremburg war crimes trials immediately following the war. The Church also quietly took many other actions during this time, all of which helped save thousands of lives. In his book, *Three Popes and the Jews,* leading Jewish author, historian, and Israeli diplomat Pinchas Lapide estimates that more than 860,000 Jews were saved due to the rescue efforts coordinated by Pope Pius XII.

During the Nazi occupation of Rome, Pius XII helped hide thousands of Jewish refugees in religious houses and in the Vatican itself, and allowed false baptismal certificates to be issued to protect them from being discovered. He also ordered other general relief efforts such as the distribution of food and clothing, as well as the melting down of sacred vessels to use their gold as a ransom for Jews held by the Nazis. The pope did all of this knowing that any defiance of Hitler's regime would mean immediate and severe retaliation, especially to those who were directly involved in such efforts.

After the war, Israel's chief rabbi formally thanked the pope for all his efforts in helping rescue so many Jews. The chief rabbi of Rome went a step further—he was baptized into the Catholic Faith on February 13, 1945, taking the baptismal name *Eugenio* (Pius XII's birth name) to show his gratitude.

When Pius XII died in 1958, Golda Meir, the Israeli delegate to the United Nations, said this about him: "When fearful martyrdom came to our people in the decade of Nazi terror, the voice of the pope was raised for the victims. The life of our times was enriched by a voice speaking out on the great moral truths above the tumult of daily conflict. We mourn a great servant of peace." Dr. Raphael Cantoni, a leader in Italy's Jewish Assistance Committee added, "Six million of my co-religionists have been murdered by the Nazis … but there would have been many more victims had it not been for the efficacious intervention of Pius XII."[14]

For more information on this important topic, you may want to check out the following resources: the film *The Scarlet and the Black* (1983) and the books *The Scarlet Pimpernel of the Vatican* by J.P. Gallagher (Coward-McCann, 1967); *Hitler, the War, and the Pope* by Ronald Rychlak (Our Sunday Visitor, 2000); and *The Defamation of Pius XII* by Ralph McInerny (St. Augustine, 2001).

Question #61

"Why does the Church collect money? It should just sell its property and give the money to the poor."

A. In fulfilling the mission given it by Christ to serve the needy, the Church needs church buildings, rectories, convents, schools, monasteries, orphanages, hospitals, and various other facilities for the care of the elderly, the poor, the sick, and the dying. On a global scale, such buildings number in the tens of thousands. Needless to say, it takes a great deal of money to operate these buildings and programs.

In the Gospel, Jesus announced that he was sent to "preach good news to the poor" (Lk 4:18). As followers of Christ, we serve him most especially when we serve the poor and the suffering. The very mission of the Church is to "walk the road Christ himself walked, a way of poverty and obedience, of service and self sacrifice" (CCC 852). Within this mission, the Church relies upon the generosity of its members in the giving of their time, talents, and resources in providing for the needs of humanity. No other institution on earth does more for the poor and the needy throughout the world than the Catholic Church. The hospitals, orphanages, and clinics run by its many religious orders, along with the efforts of Catholic relief agencies, set the standard for charitable giving to the rest of the world.

While the Church does own valuable possessions, such as priceless works of art and literature, it preserves them for the entire world to admire and appreciate. Thousands of visitors go to the Vatican every year to see these magnificent works of art and to be inspired and spiritually enriched by them. Selling such treasures to private individuals or foundations that would be free to do with them what they want could severely restrict the public's access to them. Most of these works, created by some of the most famous artists in history, were given to the Church as gifts for all to see and experience.

Can you imagine people calling for the government to close public libraries, museums, and parks so that they may be sold and the money used to build roads? Should we sell the Statue of Liberty to help pay off the national debt? Of course not. Everyone recognizes that these things exist for the benefit of every citizen.

Question #62

"How does the Church decide who becomes a saint?"

A. The process for naming a person a saint is known as *canonization*. According to the *Catechism,* "By *canonizing* some of the faithful, i.e., by solemnly proclaiming that they practiced heroic virtue and lived in fidelity to God's grace, the Church recognizes the power of the Spirit of holiness within her and sustains the hope of believers by proposing the saints to them as models and intercessors" (CCC 828). When someone is formally canonized, the Church declares a person to be in heaven and worthy of being included during the Eucharistic prayer of the Mass.

The canonization process has been changed several times over the centuries. Today, the usual process involves a ten-year period. It begins with the submission of a formal report to the Vatican's Congregation for the Causes of Saints by the bishop representing the diocese from which the person's *cause* (i.e., case) has originated. The Congregation then researches the candidate's life and decides whether or not to recommend his or her cause. If a recommendation is made, it then goes to the pope. If the pope accepts the Congregation's report, the candidate is then declared *venerable,* meaning that person is recognized as having lived a life of heroic virtue.

The next step is the process is *beatification*. This typically requires proof of at least one miracle attributed to the intercession of the candidate after his or her death. The Church conducts a thorough investigation (including the consultation of leading medical experts and scientific experts) to determine whether God truly performed a miracle through that person. Once the Church determines that a miracle did, in fact, occur, the pope (or his delegate) then declares the person *blessed* at a solemn ceremony that is usually held in St. Peter's Basilica.

The final step for formal canonization is proof of a second miracle. Once again, the Church conducts a thorough investigation. If the miracle is determined to be genuine, the pope may then declare the person a saint of the Church. When the pope canonizes someone, this act is an infallible judgment based on his authority as the successor of Peter (Mt 16:18; CCC 889). Such a declaration, therefore, must be believed and recognized by the universal Church.

Question #63

"What's the difference between a cardinal and a bishop?"

A. A cardinal (from the Latin word *cardo,* meaning "hinge") is a bishop who has been named a "prince" of the Church. Although a cardinal is given special prominence in the Church, his authority as a bishop does not increase. Cardinals wear red and are addressed as "Your Eminence."

All cardinals are appointed by the pope and are members of the College of Cardinals. There are currently about 120 cardinals, representing the important Catholic areas of the world. Most are archbishops of the largest dioceses in their countries or regions. (During his twenty-six-year pontificate, St. John Paul II made the College of Cardinals much less European and more "international" by naming cardinals from around the world.) Collectively, the cardinals assist and advise the pope in governing the Church. When a pope dies, all the world's cardinals under the age of eighty meet in Rome in a *conclave*. Behind the locked doors of the Sistine Chapel, they gather to elect the next pope.

Until modern times, prominent Catholic laymen were appointed cardinals, but now the title is given only to priests and bishops. If a priest is named, he is ordinarily consecrated a bishop before officially becoming a cardinal, but this requirement can be waived. Recently, this occurred in the United States when John Paul II named Father Avery Dulles, a prominent Jesuit theologian, a cardinal without requiring him to become a bishop.

Question #64

"How are priests chosen to be bishops?"

A. Every bishop is appointed by the pope. The process of appointing a bishop begins when the bishops of an *ecclesiastical province* (an archdiocese plus its regional dioceses; there are thirty provinces in the United States) meet each year to discuss potential candidates. The candidates, who are priests from each diocese, are presented to the archbishop of the province prior to the meeting. At the meeting, resumés of the candidates are usually distributed and qualifications discussed. The Church provides explicit guidelines about the qualities and qualifications each candidate should have.

Though specific procedures differ from province to province, a vote is usually taken to determine whether particular candidates have gained the approval of the bishops. The provincial archbishop then forwards the list of approved candidates to the pope's official representative in that country. In the United States (and many other countries), this representative is known as the *nuncio*.

The nuncio, after conducting a detailed investigation of each candidate, decides on three names to forward to the pope along with his own recommendations. Though the pope greatly relies on the advice of the nuncio, the appointment of a bishop is ultimately the pope's decision; he is free to choose anyone he wishes.

Chapter 6

THE CATHOLIC FAITH
AND OTHER RELIGIONS

Question #65

"With all the religions out there, how can we know for sure that the Catholic Faith is the right one? If ours is right, does that make everyone else's religion wrong?"

A. You're right—there are many religions to choose from, all of which claim to be the true faith. Catholics, Protestants, Jews, Muslims, Hindus, Buddhists, Taoists, Scientologists, and many others, all believe they are right and that all other religions are wrong to some degree. All offer arguments to defend their beliefs, some of which seem very persuasive. So how can we know that the Catholic Faith is true?

The truth of the Catholic Church hinges on the identity of Jesus Christ. The critical question is, "Was Jesus who he said he was?" The great Christian apologist C.S. Lewis convincingly demonstrates that Jesus could only be one of three things: a liar, a lunatic, or the Lord. Jesus cannot simply be a "nice guy." If he were just a nice guy and not God, then he was a nice guy who claimed to be something he wasn't. In other words, he was a liar. Or maybe he was just crazy—a lunatic. Lunatics often think they are people they really aren't. Jesus, though, backed up his claims of divinity with actions that were real: healings, multiplying food, walking on water, etc. Jesus could not have been a lunatic if the things he did and said were true. So if he was neither a liar nor a lunatic, then there is only one other possibility: He was who he claimed to be; he is Lord.

Through his teachings and miracles—particularly his resurrection from the dead—Jesus proved that he is the divine Son of God. This is the striking difference between Jesus and the founders of all the other major religions of the world. Jesus is the only founder of a religion who claimed to be divine. In addition, he is the only one who backed up his claim to divinity with amazing and supernatural deeds, like curing the blind and raising the dead.

If Jesus truly is God as well as man, it stands to reason that it is he who reveals the definitive truth of God. Once it has been established that Jesus is God, then one must study to see if Jesus was affiliated with any of those major religions mentioned earlier. The fact is that none of the major religions of the world—except Christianity—regard Jesus Christ as the Son of God and the Savior of the mankind.

Here's a creative exercise that may help: Imagine you are a Martian on your first visit to earth from Mars. As soon as you arrive in a cornfield to collect some data and leave some nifty crop signs, a government official named Mr. Smith captures you. Today is Monday, he tells you. He says that unless you can find the Christian church founded directly by Jesus Christ within a week, you will not be permitted to return home. He gives you a thick book, and says that you need to select from more than 35,000 Christian churches to find the true one.

Luckily, you stumble upon a Catholic bookstore, and a nice old nun, Sister Goodbook, helps you out. She tells you that if you accept that Jesus Christ founded a church, you will need to look for the one that can trace its history back to the apostles. She tells you that only one church today can validly make this claim—the Catholic Church. She gives you a Bible and tells you to read the Gospels. You go back to hide in your cornfield and, using your super reading skills by moonlight, you finish the New Testament by morning. You find that during his public ministry, Jesus gathered twelve apostles and taught them the truth he was sent to reveal. He then gave them a commission to "make disciples of all nations" (Mt 28:19), thus establishing the mission of the Church. Then, you sneak back to the bookstore and set up midnight coffee talks with the good ol' Sister Goodbook.

Throughout the week, you learn a lot and conclude your study on Sunday afternoon, after going to Mass with Sister Goodbook. In fact, Sister Goodbook helps you to write your confidential report for Mr. Smith, even giving you references from the Bible and from the *Catechism*. Your report reads like this:

Mr. Smith, when I study the history of your planet, I find that nearly all of the Christian churches of the world are "offshoots" of the one Church of Christ—the Catholic Church.

Jesus promised he would never abandon his Church, that he would remain with it "until the end of time" (Mt 28:19-20). All salvation comes from Christ through his body, the Church (see CCC 846). As the Catechism *states, it is the Catholic Church that proclaims "the fullness of faith. She bears in herself and administers the totality of the means of salvation. She is sent out to all peoples. She speaks to all men. She encompasses all times" (CCC 868). "The sole Church of Christ which in the Creed we profess to be one, holy, catholic, and apostolic ... subsists [concretely exists] in the Catholic Church" (CCC 870). For these reasons, we can be certain that the Catholic Church holds within it the fullness of the truth of God's revelation as well as the means necessary for our salvation.*

This does not mean that many elements of truth cannot be found in other Christian denominations or even in non-Christian religions. However, God calls everyone "to this catholic unity of the People of God" and, in different ways, they belong or are directed to it. This includes "the Catholic faithful, others who believe in Christ, and finally all mankind, called by God's grace to salvation" (CCC 836). God wills to "call the whole of humanity together into his Son's Church. The Church is the place where humanity must rediscover its unity and salvation" (CCC 845). Thus, to conclude my report, I firmly conclude that the Catholic Church is one Church founded by Jesus Christ.

So an objective observer (such as an alien), simply by examining the evidence in an unbiased way, would inevitably come to conclusion that the true Church of Christ is the Catholic Church.

Question #66

"The Catholic Church shouldn't be so closed-minded in claiming it is the only true faith. My friend says that a mind is like a parachute—it only works when it is open."

A. Your friend's use of the parachute analogy is interesting. But you should remind him that, most of the time, a skydiver's parachute is actually closed. A skydiver knows that to open his parachute at the wrong time—or too close to the ground—can be deadly. The purpose of a parachute is to have it open at exactly the right moment to carry the skydiver safely to the ground. So a skydiver needs to be "closed-minded" about the way a parachute is properly used.

As the great Catholic apologist G.K. Chesterton has said, the purpose of an open mind, like that of an open mouth, is to close it on something solid.[15] Once your mind has discovered the truth about something, you should "close" it. Keeping an "open mind" about things we know to be false is more than foolish; it can even be dangerous.

For example, when you get on a plane, you want the pilot to be "closed-minded" about how to fly the plane. If he decided to be "open" about the laws of aerodynamics, you would almost certainly not reach your destination safely; the plane would crash.

Similarly, when it comes to religious truth, we need to be open-minded only in our *search* for the truth. Once we find it, we need to "close" our minds and no longer be open to following what we know to be false. Jesus called himself "the Way, the Truth, and the Life" (Jn 14:6). To follow Christ is to follow the path to eternal life. Our faith is based upon the Truth, which is Jesus himself. Though other churches or religions carry within them some—or even many—elements of truth, the Catholic Church was founded by Jesus and entrusted by him with the *fullness* of truth (see CCC 851, 868, 870).

Question #67

"Is it true that the Eastern Orthodox religion is the most similar to the Catholic Faith?"

A. Yes, it is. The *Catechism* says the Eastern Orthodox Churches are "separated from the Catholic Church, yet are in imperfect but deep communion with the Catholic Church by reason of our common baptism, the profession of the Creed, and the possession of true sacraments by reason of the apostolic succession of their priesthood" (CCC glossary—*Orthodox Churches*). It further states that "this communion is so profound 'that it lacks little to attain the fullness that would permit a common celebration of the Lord's Eucharist'" (CCC 838).

Although the Eastern Orthodox Churches and the Catholic Church have much in common (such as a valid priesthood and Eucharist, the same seven sacraments, devotion to Mary, veneration of the saints, etc.), there are also a number of important differences in their beliefs. For example, the Orthodox do not accept the universal teaching authority of the pope, nor do they believe he can teach *infallibly* (i.e., without error) on matters of faith and morals. In addition, while the Orthodox faithful accept the decrees and teachings of the first seven major Church councils, ending with Nicea II in AD 787, they do not believe that decisions of later councils have any force.

Though formal separation between the Eastern Orthodox Churches and the Catholic Church has existed for more than one thousand years, recent efforts have been made toward restoring unity. St. John Paul II made reconciliation with the Orthodox a high priority during his pontificate. On numerous occasions, he used the image of the human body to describe the relationship between the Orthodox Churches and the Catholic Church, saying that "the Church must learn to breathe again with its two lungs—the Eastern one and the Western one." We must pray that one day unity may be restored.

Question #68
"Could you explain some basics about Islam?"

A. The word *Islam* in Arabic means "submission to the will of God." It is a worldwide religion, founded in the seventh century by Muhammad (AD 570–632) in what is now Saudi Arabia. It took many of its beliefs from Judaism and Christianity. The followers of Islam are known as *Muslims*, which means "one who submits."

Islam began when Muhammad claimed that *Allah* (Arabic for "God") granted him special revelations that were collected and recorded in the *Koran*, Islam's holy book. The message of Muhammad is seen by Muslims as the continuation and fulfillment of prophecies of the Old and New Testaments. Islam reveres the Bible and honors Adam, Noah, Abraham, Moses, David, Jesus, Jesus' mother, Mary, and the angels. Islam shares with Judaism and Christianity a belief in one God *(monotheism)* and in the eternal reward or punishment for one's actions. However, Islam strongly opposes such Christian doctrines as the Trinity and the divinity of Jesus. Though Islam regards Jesus as a great prophet, it does not believe he is the divine Son of God.

The principal *tenets* (or beliefs) of Islam are found in the Koran. Every Muslim is required to fulfill the following five duties: (1) Confess that "there is no God but Allah, and Muhammad is his prophet"; (2) pray five times daily, facing toward Mecca, Saudi Arabia, the holiest city of Islam; (3) give alms generously to those in need; (4) fast from sunrise to sunset during the month of Ramadan; and (5) if physically able, make a pilgrimage to Mecca once during one's lifetime.

Today, Islam is one of the world's fastest growing religions, and there are more than a billion Muslims worldwide. Followers of Islam can now be found on every continent of the globe, and the country with the largest number of Muslims is Indonesia. Muslims now make up large minorities in many European countries and in the United States as well.

Question #69

"What are some of the differences between Islam and Christianity?"

A. While some of the differences between Islam and Christianity are discussed in the previous answer, the main source of disagreement centers around the nature of God. While both religions are *monotheistic* (i.e., they believe in one God), Islam does not believe in the Trinity—God as Father, Son, and Holy Spirit. They believe that the notion of Three Persons in the Trinity runs counter to the unity and oneness of God's nature. In addition, Muslims' view God as utterly *transcendent*, i.e., completely above and apart from the created world.

So it would be impossible for him to have a son, much less one who is also a man, born of a woman. Although Islam honors Jesus as a prophet, he is considered merely a man, nothing more. He is not even considered the greatest of the prophets. Muhammad has that role, and it is he who is seen as God's apostle to mankind.

Unlike the Catholic Faith, Islam has no sacraments and no priesthood. It also lacks a hierarchical structure, though it does have *clerics* (religious leaders) who lead the faithful in public prayer and offer guidance and direction. These clerics, however, have no universal teaching authority.

Islam believes in one all-just, all-powerful God who created the world and man. It insists on obedience to his will and promises salvation and immortality to believers. But unlike Christianity, it does not recognize Jesus as the divine Son of God. For Islam, it is Muhammad who completes the prophetic line that brings the law of God to man.

If you want to learn more about Islam, check out the question-and-answer book *Inside Islam: A Guide for Catholics* (Ascension, 2003), by Daniel Ali and Robert Spencer.

Question #70

"Why don't the Jewish people accept Jesus as the Messiah?"

A. To begin with, we need to remember that there were many Jews during Jesus' public ministry and afterward who *did* accept Jesus as the Messiah. All of the twelve apostles were Jews, as were nearly all of Jesus' disciples and many early converts. Many of these early Jewish Christians were martyred for the Faith—for example, St. Stephen, St. Barnabas, and St. Paul. Throughout the two-thousand–year history of Christianity, many Jews have come to accept Jesus and have converted to Christianity. A famous example from the twentieth century is Edith Stein, who became Catholic and later, a Carmelite nun. During World War II, she died in a Nazi concentration camp. She was recently canonized and is now revered as a saint of the Church.

The Old Testament teaches that the Jews are God's Chosen People. After the sin of Adam and Eve, it was through the Jewish nation that a Savior, the Messiah, was promised. The entire Old Testament is the story of the Jews preparing for the coming of the Messiah. Under the leadership of powerful kings such as David and Solomon, the Jewish people became a great nation. But, due to repeated disobedience to God on the part of the kings and the people, they were repeatedly conquered and oppressed by various enemies.

At the time of the birth of Jesus, the Holy Land was under the occupation of the Roman Empire, and the Jews longed to be freed from the hands of their captors. Many expected that the Messiah would be a military or political leader who would drive out their Roman enemies and restore the Jewish nation to its previous glory and power. When Jesus did arrive, he did not fit the profile of such a leader, and when he was eventually condemned to death, most of the Jews rejected him.

From the perspective of the gospel, though, Jesus did not come to restore the Jewish nation of the past, but to establish the kingdom of God for all peoples and nations.

The Old Testament is full of signs and prophecies of how the Messiah would be recognized. It reveals he would be born of a virgin (Is 7:14) in Bethlehem (Mi 5:1-2), enter Jerusalem on a donkey (Zec 9:9), be betrayed for thirty pieces of silver (Zec 11:12), be persecuted and condemned to death (Is 53:3-4, 7-9), give his life as an offering for sin (Is 53:10), have lots cast for his garments (Ps 22:18), be pierced for our sins (Is 53:5), be raised from the dead, and not experience corruption of the body (Ps 16:10). In spite of these clear indications in the Scriptures, many of the Jews of Jesus' time were expecting a powerful, earthly Messiah. It is not surprising, then, that they many of them failed to recognize their true King when he came into their midst.

Question #71

"Is it OK for me to go with my friend to his non-Catholic church?"

A. While it is OK for you to attend a non-Catholic church occasionally, a few important principles need to be kept in mind.

First, as Catholics we are required to attend Mass every Sunday, as well as on holy days of obligation (CCC 2180–2182). Attending a non-Catholic service does not fulfill this obligation, so it is necessary to go to Mass either on Saturday night or on Sunday.

Secondly, if we attend a non-Catholic service, we are not permitted to receive communion, even if we are invited to do so by the pastor. Receiving communion would be saying that we are in full Christian communion with their church—which we are not. Taking communion would also imply that their "Eucharist" is the real presence of

Jesus—which it is not. The only exceptions to this rule are the Eastern Orthodox Churches, which *do* have a valid priesthood and Eucharist. If we are visiting an area or country (e.g., Greece or Russia) in which access to a Catholic church is limited, we may attend an Orthodox Liturgy and receive Communion (see CCC 1399). But this is an unusual situation.

Third, as Catholics, we believe that the fullness of the Christian truth *subsists* (concretely exists) in the Catholic Church (see CCC 816). As much as we love and respect our non-Catholic brothers and sisters, there are some Protestant churches that are anti-Catholic and seek to draw Catholics away from their faith. Before attending your friend's church, I would ask him the following questions: "Have you ever heard any anti-Catholic statements by the pastor or members of your church? Does your church believe that Catholics are true Christians? Does your church try to convert Catholics?" The answers to these questions should help you decide whether it would be a good idea to attend his or her church.

Question #72

"Why can't my Protestant friend receive the Eucharist when he comes to Mass with me?"

A. This is a frequent source of confusion and tension in the Church today. Many Catholics have a hard time understanding why the Church does not permit non-Catholics to receive the Eucharist, particularly at special occasions such as weddings and funerals. This is all the more difficult because many Protestant churches—perhaps including your friend's church—allow anyone who is a baptized Christian to receive communion during their services. These churches see communion as a sign of unity among Christians, and so they encourage everyone to receive.

St. Paul, in his first letter to Corinthians, writes that "because there is one bread, we who are many are one body, for we all partake of the one bread" (1 Cor 10:17). Catholics also believe that the Eucharist is a sign of Christian unity (see CCC 1323), but we need to remember what the Eucharist truly *is* and *why* it is the source of unity.

As Catholics, we believe the Eucharist truly contains the Body, Blood, Soul, and Divinity of Jesus under the form of bread and wine (see CCC 1375, 1376). When we receive Communion, the priest, deacon, or Eucharistic minister says, "The Body of Christ," and we respond, "Amen." *Amen* is a Hebrew word meaning "truly" or "it is so." It is a confirmation or expression of belief. When we receive the Eucharist, we accept with conviction that it is truly the Body of Christ.

Though many Protestant churches have communion and may even refer to it as "Eucharist," the majority of them do not share our belief in the real presence. Most view Communion as merely a *symbol* of Christ's presence among us. These churches, as the *Catechism* notes, "have not preserved the proper reality of the Eucharistic mystery in its fullness ... it is for this reason that Eucharistic intercommunion with these communities is not possible" (CCC 1400). Therefore, to permit our non-Catholic friends to say "Amen" and receive something they do not truly believe in would be inappropriate or even blasphemous. And even if they do believe that the Eucharist is the Body and Blood of Christ, they do not possess the unity with his true Church that reception of the Eucharist implies.

Normally, only Catholics may receive the Eucharist. The only exception to this rule is if a grave necessity arises (e.g., someone in danger of death). In such a circumstance, a non-Catholic Christian "who asks of it of their own free will, provided they give evidence of holding the Catholic faith regarding [this] sacrament" may receive the Eucharist with the permission of the local bishop (CCC 1401).[16]

The Eucharist is the very heart of the Church's life (see CCC 2177). Therefore, only members of the Church can fully appreciate, embrace, and love it as their own. The good news is that God invites *everyone* on earth to become a member of the Church and share in the one Eucharist.

Though not all may fully participate, everyone is invited to the Lamb's Supper. Many Catholic parishes encourage non-Catholics to approach the altar at Communion, not to receive the Eucharist, but rather a blessing. If your friend is comfortable with this and your parish offers such blessings, it might reduce some of the awkwardness he or she may feel at being the only one left in the pew during Communion.

To receive a blessing, your friend should get into a Communion line of a priest or deacon because lay Eucharistic ministers cannot give a blessing. You should teach your friend to make a visible symbol for the priest or deacon to see that signals a desire for a blessing, not Communion. Holding one's arms across the chest in the form of an "X," as well as slightly bowing the head are two fairly universally recognized symbols for such a desire. Receiving a blessing is a good thing, just as many small children receive one as they wait to reach the age of their first Communion. This practice is also a good idea if one is in the state of mortal sin and unable to receive Communion. In this way, a non-Catholic, as well a Catholic can make a *spiritual communion* with Jesus.

Question #73

"A Seventh-day Adventist friend says that since Saturday is the Jewish Sabbath, Christians should worship on this day rather than on Sunday. How do I answer her?"

A. Your friend is half right. In accordance with the commands of the Old Testament, the Jews celebrate their Sabbath on the seventh day of the week, Saturday. However, from the very first days of the Church, early Christians gathered to worship on Sunday, the first day of the week, because Jesus rose from the dead on Easter Sunday. St. Justin Martyr, writing in the year AD 155, wrote that, "On the day we call the day of the sun [Sunday], all who dwell in the city or country gather in the same place" to celebrate the Eucharist (see CCC 1345).[17]

The *Catechism* explains that the Sabbath was "the day to be kept holy to the praise and worship of God. Just as the seventh day or Sabbath completes the first creation, so ... Sunday ... is celebrated as the 'holy day' by Christians ... Thus the Christian observance of Sunday fulfills the commandment to remember and keep holy the Sabbath day" (CCC glossary—*Sabbath*).

As the book of Acts notes, the non-Jewish Christians held their religious meetings on "the first day of the week," which is Sunday (Acts 20:7). With the disappearance of "Jewish" Christian churches, this quickly became the norm for all Christians. St. Ignatius of Antioch, a disciple of St. John the Apostle, speaks of Christians "no longer observing the Sabbath but living in the observance of the Lord's Day, in which our life is blessed by him and by his death" (see CCC 2175).

So the Seventh-Day Adventists' belief that Saturday is the "true Sabbath" for Christians is clearly contrary to the practice of the early Church. This view is a nineteenth-century innovation and is rejected by all other Protestant churches, who agree with the Catholic Church that Sunday is the appropriate day for Christians to worship the Lord.

Question #74

"My best friend is a Jehovah's Witness. How can I tell her that her faith is not the one true faith without losing her friendship?"

A. Your situation is actually very common. Many Catholics today have non-Catholic friends, and it is sometimes difficult to share the truths of our faith in a confident, clear, and charitable way.

Although your friend, as a Jehovah's Witness, has religious beliefs that significantly differ from the Catholic Faith, there are things you can affirm about her faith, including her desire to know the truth, her conviction, and her zeal to evangelize. In talking to your friend, concentrate on those areas that you and she can agree on before you get into the differences. Avoid being confrontational or argumentative. As much as you may win the argument, you don't accomplish anything if your friend is offended and walks away.

Remember that only the Holy Spirit can bring about a real change of heart. This is why prayer is so important. Before talking to your friend, be sure to put the situation into God's hands. Also, focus on one issue at a time. This way, the conversation is not overwhelming and there is also time for reflection, thought, and prayer.

Lastly, we must be willing to love our friends even if they don't share our beliefs. Pray to the Holy Spirit for wisdom and guidance' and know that he will show you the way. Pray that your friend will be open to the workings of the Spirit so that one day he or she may come to know and embrace the fullness of truth. You would be surprised how many people have been converted to the Catholic faith by the witness of their friends.

Question #75

"Why do Jehovah's Witnesses say that God's real name is *Jehovah?*"

A. The reason has to do with a mistake made in the pronunciation of the name *Yahweh*, the name of God revealed to Moses at the burning bush on Mt. Sinai (Ex 3:14). The Old Testament was written in Hebrew during a period when no vowels were used in writing. Therefore, the name *Yahweh* was actually written in the Old Testament as YHWH. Over time, out of reverence for the sacredness of God's name, it became the practice of the Hebrews not to pronounce it. Instead, they substituted the name *Adonai*, meaning *Lord.*

In order to emphasize this, Hebrew Scripture scholars added vowel symbols into Old Testament texts to indicate to the reader that the name *Adonai* was to be used in place of YHWH. These vowel symbols were usually written below the consonants of YHWH to indicate their correct sound.

Centuries later, a number of Christian scholars, studying the Old Testament, mistakenly combined the consonants of *Yahweh* (YHWH) with the vowels of *Adonai* to produce what sounds like *Yahowah*. Throughout the evolution of the English language, the letter *j* was used interchangeably with the letter *y* (just like the letter *v* with the letter *w*). Thus, what sounded like *Yahowah* became popularly written and pronounced as *Jehovah*.

This spelling actually found its way into early English editions of the Bible, including the popular King James Version used by many Protestants. Later versions of the King James and most other English translations substitute LORD whenever YHWH appears. But Jehovah's Witnesses (and some other Protestant Christians) continue using the name *Jehovah* despite its mistaken origin.

Question #76

"Would it be sinful for a Catholic to leave the Faith and join a non-Catholic church?"

A. Doing something contrary to God's will is always objectively wrong. The *Catechism* reminds us that God calls everyone to the "catholic unity of the People of God" found in the Catholic Church (see CCC 836, 845). This is because the Church possesses the fullness of truth and the ordinary means of grace necessary for growth in holiness. However, this does not mean that everyone who leaves the Catholic Church is necessarily guilty of sin. It depends on whether the person knows—or should know—that God wills the person to belong to the Catholic Church (see CCC 846–848).

Some people who leave the Catholic Church may not realize what they are doing is wrong, hence they may not be held accountable. On the other hand, someone who knows better—i.e., who knows in his heart that God wills him to belong to Christ's Church and rejects it—may very well be held accountable. However, we ourselves cannot judge such people. Only God can truly know the heart of a person. We should always pray for these people in the hope that they will come to see the truth and return to the loving embrace of God's holy family, the Church.

Question #77

"My sister is a fallen-away Catholic who now attends an Episcopal church. She says that her church believes in the real presence of Jesus in the Eucharist, just as Catholics do. Is she right?"

A. To begin with, you should be careful using the phrase "real presence" when talking with non-Catholics. Many Christians accept that Jesus is "really present" in the Eucharist (or "communion," as they often call it), but they mean something different than the Catholic Church's understanding of this phrase. Some Christian denominations that celebrate communion regularly—Episcopalians and Lutherans, for example—believe Jesus is "really present" *along with* the bread and wine. This doctrine is called *consubstantiation.* Catholics, on the other hand, believe that the bread and wine are literally and completely *changed* into the Body, Blood, Soul, and Divinity of Jesus (see CCC 1374–1377). This is known as *transubstantiation.*

The key is not so much what any particular Christian denomination may *believe* about communion, but what they actually *possess.* Only the Catholic Church (along with the Eastern Orthodox Churches) has valid orders, i.e., priests who are validly ordained by bishops who can trace a line of succession all the way back to the original apostles. It is this power that enables the Church to follow the instruction of its founder, Jesus Christ, who desired that his sacrifice for us on earth be memorialized through the ages by virtue of the words of the priest, "This is my body ... this is my blood." It is at this precise moment during the Holy Sacrifice of the Mass (referred to as the *consecration*) that the bread and wine cease to be bread and wine, and truly become the Body and Blood of Jesus (see CCC 1377).

This is what is meant by the "real presence" of Jesus. Only a validly ordained priest, through the power of Christ given to him by the bishop (a successor of the apostles), can *confect* (bring about) the real presence of Jesus in the Eucharist. Because the Episcopal Church does not have valid holy orders as recognized by the Catholic Church, it does not have the faculties necessary to enact the real presence in the Eucharist, no matter how close to ours their theological concept of the Eucharist may appear to be.

Chapter 7

CATHOLIC LIVING

Question #78

"What is our purpose for being here in this world?"

A. This is the most important question in life; it is also the shortest answer in this book. Sometimes the most profound questions have the simplest answers!

In short, God created us to know, love, and serve him in this life, so we can be happy with him forever in the next life (see CCC 356). Since our ultimate purpose is eternal happiness in heaven, we must say "yes" to God's grace in this life by loving him and by loving our neighbor as ourselves.

Question #79

"Each year, I go on an incredible retreat that helps me really feel close to God, but in the months that follow, the feeling goes away. What can I do to keep that 'Jesus high' all year long?"

A. When the apostles Peter, James, and John were on the mountain with Jesus during his transfiguration, it was such a powerful experience for Peter that he suggested they put up tents and stay there for good (see Mt 17:1-6; Mk 9:1-8; Lk 9:28-36). But Jesus had other plans. He knew that the people "down below" needed to be ministered to, and that he needed to continue on the road to Calvary. It is no coincidence that the same three apostles who were present there on the mountaintop were also present in the Garden of Gethsemane with Jesus during his agony.

Life is not simply about "highs," about "feeling good." It also involves "lows"—suffering and struggle. It is when we return to the valley that our faith is most real; it is in the desert that Christ forms us and raises us up to be men and women of God. Our walk with the Lord will have "Jesus highs" from time to time, but our faithfulness to him is demonstrated when those feelings are not present and we still decide to stand with him. When the good feelings of a great spiritual experience are taken from us, we are asked, "Do I love God for *his* sake or for the good feelings I get when I am with him?" When the excitement dies down and we still walk with him, that is when our faith actually grows the most.

To keep the flame of his grace alive, you should regularly receive the sacraments of reconciliation and Holy Eucharist—and the more often the better. These are fountains of grace. There is a story about a young man at a bonfire. He was standing next to a priest and they began talking. The young man asked the priest why it was necessary to go to Mass each week. Without saying a word, the priest took some prongs and pulled a red-hot coal from the fire. He sat it on the sand a few feet from the fire, and they watched it become cold and gray within seconds. The young man got the point. If you stay away from Jesus by skipping the sacraments, your spiritual life will quickly lose the "high" that you felt on retreat. You can't keep a "Jesus high" without Jesus!

Also, set a prayer time each day—and don't miss it. Read the Bible, and learn from the lessons it teaches. Throughout your life, become close to Our Lady. The Rosary is a powerful tool that can help us stay close to God.

Question #80

"What is the best way to determine God's will for my life? I know God speaks through prayer, but how do I know when it's really God speaking to me or just my own thoughts?"

A. Some people think that if they become holy, they will always know exactly what God has planned for them. But God wants us to walk by faith. His will, as it pertains to our future, is often hidden from us. Have you ever seen someone working on a needlepoint quilt? The back of the quilt often looks like an absolute mess, with threads sticking out all over the place. Sometimes in life, this is all we see and wonder what God is up to. In time, we will see the beautiful design—"the other side of the quilt"—that he has been working on. During these times, he asks for us to be still and know that he is God (Ps 46:9-11).

For this reason, holiness mainly consists in submitting to God's will in the present moment rather than in knowing things before they happen. As the prophet Isaiah tells us, "For as the heavens are higher than the earth, so are my ways higher than your ways and my thoughts than your thoughts" (Is 55:9). It might be a good idea for us to admit this and say, "God, you know me, and you know that if a door even looks partially open, I'll ram my head into it repeatedly until it opens or is bolted shut. So, to prevent any further injuries, could you please bolt the door shut or open it wide?"

Here are a few practical tips to try that can help you hear God's voice more clearly:

1. *Get a spiritual director.* Consider asking a trusted priest (or even a wise and faithful adult who is trained in spiritual matters) to be your spiritual director. Having a spiritual director can really help you sort things out and discern God's will for your life. You should meet regularly with your director to pray and talk with him about the direction of your spiritual life.

2. *Receive the sacrament of reconciliation (confession).* Sin is the primary obstacle that confuses us, distracts us, and plugs our ears with junk that keeps us from hearing God's voice. Getting to the sacrament of reconciliation regularly can be a great way to "unclog" our ears, clear our minds, and make our hearts ready to receive God's guidance in our lives. If your spiritual director is a priest, using this time to go to confession will help you begin anew and gain additional grace.

3. *Talk out loud.* Talk to a good and faithful friend about what you think God may be telling you. Bouncing it off someone you trust can be very helpful. You may learn that the idea is worth a deeper look through more attention and prayer, or you may discover that it is probably not from God at all.

4. *Keep a prayer journal.* Keeping a regular "spiritual diary" can help you to look at where you are traveling in your spiritual journey. Even writing just a few sentences each day or each week can help you keep track of what God is doing in your life, what he is trying to say to you, and where he may be leading you. If you think God is telling you something, it just might be important enough to write down!

5. *Pray the Scriptures.* Sometimes you can read the Psalms or some other book of the Bible and be astounded at how the author went through the same thing you are going through now! Reading and praying the words of Scripture can be a great guide for gaining spiritual— and even practical—wisdom.

6. *Practice listening.* Hearing God's voice is not always easy, especially in today's world of constant noise, distraction, and stimulation filled with music, cell phones, TV, and computers. If you want to truly learn to hear the voice of God, you must, like anything else, practice, practice, practice ... a lot! Try to find a quiet place in your room or in a nearby church or Adoration chapel where you can spend regular time in complete silence, only echoing quietly the words of Samuel, "Speak, for thy servant hears" (1 Sam 3:10). It will be hard at first, or for a while, but if you can learn to "Be still, and know I am God" (Ps 46:10), then you will be quiet enough, settled enough, and open enough to hear God when he speaks to you.

Always remember that God loves you and has a plan for you (see Jer 29:11-14). Many times, we overanalyze things and fail to see how simple and perfect his ways are. Pray for peace and wisdom and he will grant these to you.

Fr. Michael Scanlan, TOR, has written a great book on this topic called *What Does God Want? A Practical Guide to Making Decisions* (Our Sunday Visitor, 1996).

Question #81

"How can I know if God is calling me to the priesthood or religious life?"

A. Each of us is called by God to live our lives in a particular way. The word "vocation" comes from the Latin *vocare,* which means "to call." God calls each of us to a particular state in life that he has destined for us before we were ever born. It is within this vocation that we discover who we are and what we are meant to be, and how we are to achieve a life in service to God and others. This divine plan for our lives offers us the best means of fulfilling our ultimate purpose in this life, and it prepares us for eternal life as well.

There are three vocations to which God calls people: marriage, consecrated life, and single life. They all are fantastic ways to live and love God. But how do we discover which one is our *personal* vocation? The discernment of our vocation begins by saying "yes" to whatever God wants for us in our lives. So the first step is to be completely open to his will.

It may be obvious, but God calls most people to marriage. Some people think that the word "vocation" is used only for a calling to the priesthood or religious life, but this is not the full picture. Marriage, consecrated life, and single life are all true vocations. In fact, we need marriage in order to have the other two!

Our discernment begins by trusting God. If we believe that God loves us and wants what is best for us, then we can trust that he will guide us to our true vocation. Trust requires being open to his grace. A strong and active prayer life, along with frequent reception of the sacraments (especially the Holy Eucharist and reconciliation), is essential in helping you discern your vocation. Be patient; have confidence that God will lead you in a direction that you will ultimately desire for yourself. Whatever your vocation is, God will put that desire into your heart and give you peace with it.

Because we grow up in families rather than in monasteries, convents, or rectories, we generally have a good idea of what married life is all about. But we may not know much about the priesthood or religious life. So if you think you may be called to the priesthood or religious life, you need to speak with a priest or sister who can offer you good advice and direction, someone who can clue you in to what this vocation is all about. Most dioceses have a vocations office staffed by people who are eager to answer any questions you may have. Also, most seminaries and religious orders have an "open house" day when anyone can visit the seminary or religious community. This is a great opportunity to meet and talk to seminarians, priests, and religious, and to ask them questions about their lives.

Don't be afraid to follow where you think God may be calling you. In prayer, ask Jesus to provide you with wisdom and guidance, and he will lead you to where he wants you to go. You may be surprised how God works in providing certain signs and signals, in both big ways and small, to help you discover your vocation, whatever it may be. Your vocation is certainly nothing to be afraid of! As a good priest once said, it is good to remember that "God does not call the qualified. He qualifies those whom he calls."

Question #82

"The idea of evangelizing seems pretty intimidating to me. Do you have any suggestions on how to start sharing my faith without making a fool of myself?"

A. Every Catholic is called to spread the message of the gospel, but you may not be comfortable doing so. However, it may surprise you to learn that there are many ways of spreading the Faith, including some things you may already be doing but weren't even aware of. While not everyone is called to spread the Good News of the gospel on a street corner or in a foreign country, every Catholic can begin sharing the Good News. This evangelization can be done without even leaving your home, school, or office. Here are a few tips—some "do's" and "don'ts"—to help make your efforts at spreading our Catholic Faith more effective:

Some "Don'ts"

1. *Don't* think you need a theology degree or to travel across the globe to spread the Faith. The patron saint of foreign missions, St. Thérèse of Lisieux, never even left her convent! Her prayers and "little way" of doing small things with great love helped strengthen those working "in the field" to spread the gospel.

2. *Don't* expect someone to be converted according to your personal timetable. St. Monica prayed for fifteen years for her wayward and promiscuous son. Today, we know him as St. Augustine. It is easy to forget that God wants a person's conversion much more than you do. Look to God's patience as a model, reminding

yourself of how patient he has been with you over the years.

3. *Don't* be confrontational. Being passionate does not mean being overly aggressive. You may win the argument but could end up losing a soul.

4. *Don't* judge the success of a conversation by how many times you've "stumped" the other person.

5. *Don't* give in to discouragement if your efforts do not immediately yield the desired results. In Acts 20:9, St. Paul is preaching the gospel to Eutychus, and Eutychus dozes off and falls out of a window, plummeting to his death. If the preaching of an apostle can end in disaster, we have no grounds for discouragement if we don't see instant conversions. Conversions happen in God's time, not ours. Incidentally, after St. Paul prayed over him, Eutychus came back to life (see Acts 20:10-12).

Some "Do's"

1. *Pray.* Pray *before, during,* and *after* each opportunity you have to lead others to Jesus and the Church (1 Thess 5:17). Prayer is ammunition for conversions. Without prayer, you'll be pulling the trigger but shooting blanks.

2. *Be patient.* "And the Lord's servant must not be quarrelsome but kindly to everyone, an apt teacher, forbearing, correcting his opponents with gentleness. God may perhaps grant that they will repent and come to know the truth" (2 Tim 2:24-25). Be calm in your conversations so that you display the peace of Christ.

3. *Be creative.* Be creative in your evangelization efforts. For example, keep good Catholic books around, as well as chastity booklets, like *Pure Love.*

4. *Preach through your actions.* "Preach the gospel at all times, and when necessary, use words." This quote, attributed to St. Francis of Assisi, points out that our good lives can be even more powerful than our words in sharing our Catholic faith. Effective evangelization begins with our own daily conversion to Christ.

5. *Practice humility.* When you don't know the answer to a question, say so. When others stump you, tell them that you will get back to them (not back *at* them), and set a time to meet again. Then do some homework and bring them the answer.

You will notice that the common theme running throughout most of these "do's" and "don'ts" is humility. The more you live with the gentleness and courage of Christ in your life, the more you will draw others to him.

Question #83

"What if a teenager has been raised in the Catholic faith but still does not believe in it? Would it be right for his parents to force it on him?"

A. Strictly speaking, no one—including parents—can *force* someone else to believe; faith must be a free act. However, it is the responsibility of parents to raise their children in the Faith, to help them learn about it, and to help them actively live it. This responsibility includes making sure that their children attend Mass on Sundays and holy days of obligation, that they receive the sacraments (especially penance), and that they are raised with an understanding of Church teaching and what it means to be Catholic.

This is why we are baptized as infants. Baptism brings us into the family of God, and this essential act requires parents and godparents to make sure their children are brought up and nurtured in the Catholic Faith (see CCC 1251). Until adulthood, children must obey their parents (unless they command things that are sinful). When children become adults, they gain the privilege of making their own decisions—including decisions regarding ownership of their religious faith and religious practices—independent of their parents. It is important to remember that as long as the child lives in the family home, parents have every right to establish "rules of the house" and to ensure that immoral activity is not occurring under their roof. Even as adults, sons and daughters should continue to give their parents the respect that is owed them (see CCC 2217).

Teens often underestimate the wisdom of their parents. Mark Twain once remarked that when he was in high school, he considered his father to be an ignorant man. After Twain had come home from college, though, he was amazed at how much his father had learned in just four years! In reality, his father had not changed. Mark Twain had grown older and finally recognized the wisdom his father had already possessed.

Question #84

"Sometimes non-Catholics accuse me of not being a Christian because I am Catholic. How can I respond to this?"

A. For the first one thousand years of Christianity, there was one Christian Church—the *Catholic* (or "universal") Church. It was not until AD 1054 that the Christian Churches of the East broke away from the Catholic Church,

118 *Did Jesus Have a Last Name?*

thus forming Eastern Orthodoxy. Then, in the sixteenth century, the Protestant Reformation brought about yet another, much more radical split from the Catholic Church, this time involving many of the countries of Europe. This ultimately led to the thousands of individual Christian denominations that exist today.

There is no denying that there are some fundamental theological differences between the many non-Catholic churches and the Catholic Church. However, on the whole, most conservative Protestant denominations have much in common with the Catholic Faith. For example, doctrines related to the Trinity, the Incarnation, original sin, the redeeming work of Christ, the Resurrection, the necessity of baptism, salvation, and morality is virtually the same.

Many of the people you encounter who do not consider Catholics to be Christians are simply speaking out if ignorance. Don't let them agitate you. They may have been raised with an anti-Catholic prejudice or with a false understanding of what Catholics really believe. Remain charitable and Christ-like in all your interactions with them. The best way to convince them is through your own Christian witness.

Question #85

"When I discuss matters of faith on the Internet, I get frustrated because some fundamentalist Christians say that Catholics aren't real Christians. I end up feeling guilty about arguing with them."

A. There is nothing wrong with having a good, healthy discussion—or even debate—with someone. But the Bible teaches us to be gentle as we share our faith (see

2 Tim 2:24). It is not good to lose one's temper and become uncharitable. If you find that happening, it is a good idea to take a break and pray, asking the Lord to bless your words with his peace, patience, gentleness, and love.

There is such a thing as "holy anger" (also called "righteous anger"), such as when Jesus knocked over all the moneychangers' tables at the Temple. When dealing with non-Catholic Christians, though, be careful if you get angry often. Remember that they often have countless misconceptions about the Catholic Faith, so be patient and explain the truth to them gently and charitably. They will probably ask you questions you can't answer right away. When this happens, be honest—tell them you don't know, but that you will get them an answer as soon as possible. Then, go to a reliable teacher of the Faith or a solidly Catholic Internet resource such as Catholic.com to get the answer.

Question #86

"Is it OK for Catholics listen to contemporary Christian music?"

A. In general, yes. Some contemporary Christian music is performed by Catholic artists, but most of it is by evangelical Protestant musicians. A Catholic may listen to Christian music, most of which is encouraging, inspirational, worshipful, and not harmful in any way. However, some songs do have erroneous theology, perhaps promoting a false concept of salvation or of the "rapture."

As a Catholic listener, you need to be careful about what the lyrics are saying. For example, there is a Christian song out there that has a good intention of wanting to unite Christians. Unfortunately, the lyrics also denounce

the use of creeds. There were Christians in the first
centuries that, while dying as martyrs, scrawled the word
Credo ("I believe") into the ground with their own blood.
Their witness and love for the truth should inspire us to
achieve real Christian unity through truth, not through the
abandonment of creeds.

If you're not familiar with contemporary Christian music,
you may want to check out the most popular bands,
songs, and latest info on-line at the *CCM Magazine*
website: ccmcom.com.

Question #87

**"My boyfriend isn't really into church. What should I
do to help him with his relationship with God?"**

A. If you want to draw someone closer to God, step
number one is getting closer to him yourself. Pray for your
boyfriend, and strive to live a good Christian life, one that
shows the joy and peace you have found in following
Jesus. As St. Francis of Assisi said, "Preach the gospel at all
times, and when necessary, use words."

Regarding some practical things you can do, number
one is to continue and intensify your prayers for his
conversion, especially when you are at Mass or by
saying a Rosary for him. You may also want to include
doing little sacrifices or penances for him, like fasting
or performing some act of charity and offering that as a
prayer for him. Also, see if there is a local Catholic youth
group nearby, or attend a Sunday youth Mass. Finally,
read up on your faith. He may have some legitimate
questions or objections to the Catholic Faith, and so it is
wise to find answers for him.

Question #88

"When trying to convince someone you are telling the truth, is 'swearing to God' an allowable practice?"

A. If people generally know you to be an honest person, then a genuine promise on your part should be enough for them to believe you are telling the truth. Normally, "swearing to God"—which is called taking an *oath*—should be limited to solemn occasions and done only when necessary. For example, if we are called to testify in a court of law, we are asked to swear upon the Bible that we will be honest in our testimony. In order for an oath to be a holy act, we must have a good reason for taking the oath, be convinced of the truthfulness of what we are swearing to, and not take it to facilitate our doing wrong. If you call on God to bear witness to a lie, you commit a sin called *perjury.* This is not only wrong in the American court system, it is wrong in God's "court" as well—it is seriously sinful.

Question #89

"How do I learn to pray?"

A. First, realize that we are not born knowing how to pray; we need to ask God to teach us. Then, take a look at Mark 1:35—Jesus gets up really early in the morning and goes into solitude to pray. This shows us that there is wisdom in planning a *time* and *place* to pray.

If you are serious about working out, you will have a specific gym, a workout partner, a time to hit the weights, and a proper diet. So, where is your spiritual gym? Obviously, regular attendance at Mass is vitally important. There can be no higher expression of prayer offered than that of the Mass. When you are not at church, it is always a good idea to try to find a place at home or in your room that you can set aside for prayer. Maybe you could place a standing crucifix, a candle, or a picture of the Sacred Heart of Jesus there.

Who is your spiritual workout partner? Do you have a good priest that you go to for confession? Having a priest with whom you feel comfortable and can share honestly can be a huge benefit to your prayer life. Many of the saints have written about the power of having a spiritual director. Spiritual directors can help guide you in your spiritual life and give you advice on how to overcome the areas of prayer that are the most difficult for you.

Also, are you close to the Blessed Mother? The Lord has given us a great gift in his own mother. Imagine that your father asked you to clean your room and take your dirty clothes to the laundry room. You scoop them all up and shuffle across the house, dropping a sock here and some pants there. When you get to the laundry room, you realize that you dropped half the pile along the way. You turn around, and there is your mother, carrying the rest behind you. That's what Our Lady does in prayer. She's like the perfect prayer partner that prays with us and for us to bring our needs to her Son. She'll take you straight to Jesus.

Do you have a set time that you pray? If you're a morning person, you may want to get up ten minutes earlier for prayer. If you are more of a night person, then pray after dinner. But be careful about pushing prayer time to right before you go to bed. Night prayers are great, but if you want some quality time with God, make sure to do it at a time when you are fully alert. Whatever time you choose, be consistent!

When starting your prayer, ask the Holy Spirit to come and bless your prayer time. Then, pause to become aware of God's presence: (1) all around you; (2) in the Eucharist during Mass and in the tabernacle; (3) in your soul; and (4) in heaven, watching you pray. This brief recollection may help you to focus on the reality of how near he is to you. Sometimes we drift off, because we don't realize how closely God listens to our every word. I once heard of a saint that said, "How do you expect God to listen to you if you are not even listening to yourself?"

As we have mentioned, the key to getting in "good prayer shape" is consistency. Set aside ten minutes at the beginning of a day or at night and watch how your spiritual life deepens. Also, while this "working out" analogy is a good one, we need to remember that prayer is much more than just spiritual exercise. It is an intimate living relationship with God. Praying one *Our Father* with attention, devotion, and love is worth more than praying a hundred of them in a distracted and rushed way. In the words of St. Teresa of Avila, prayer is "to be alone with him who we know loves us."[18]

Question #90

"Is it sinful to accuse someone of doing something that is wrong?"

A. No, charity and justice sometimes require us to point out another's wrongdoing. This is called *fraternal correction*. We do this out of love for the person, so that they might repent and fix the harm they may have caused by their sin. In the Gospel, Jesus teaches us that we should "go and tell [your brother] his fault, between you and him alone. If he listens to you, you have gained your brother" (Mt 18:15-17). And we should always be loving and kind when we confront the person (see CCC 1829). As St. Paul says, "If a person is caught in some transgression, you who are spiritual should correct that one in gentle spirit, looking to yourself, so that you also may not be tempted. Bear one another's burdens, and so fulfill the law of Christ" (Gal 6:1-2).

We must be careful in not being too judgmental about another's sins. Jesus cautions us about finding fault with others, especially as they compare to our own shortcomings: "For with the judgment you pronounce you will be judged, and the measure you give will be the measure you get. Why do you see the speck that is in your brother's eye, but do not notice the log in your own eye? You hypocrite, first take the log out of your own eye, and then you will see clearly to take the speck out of your brother's eye" (Mt 7:2-5). So we will be judged by God on how we judge others. None of us is perfect, and we should correct others the way we would want to be corrected.

Of course, fraternal correction applies to "everyday" types of faults and sins. If someone you know has committed a serious crime, however, you should inform the proper authorities rather than confronting the person yourself. Reporting a person you know to the police may take great courage on your part, but you may end up saving another person or society from great harm.

Question #91

"How should I deal with someone who is dying?"

A. Hopefully, you are asking about how you should act around a person who is dying, not how you can personally cope with the death of someone. How you cope with losing a loved one is a matter for prayer and counseling. In reference to caring for the dying, you should treat the person with selfless compassion, like St. Teresa of Calcutta (Mother Teresa) did. Try to see Jesus in the person who is suffering. Always remember that the person is a child of God who is made in his image and likeness. You should see value in his sufferings and help him see this value. You should never despair or let him despair. Speak to him about the glory he will receive *for all eternity* when he dies.

If the person has been led to believe that killing himself—through euthanasia or assisted suicide—is a better way out, you should reinforce that God loves him more than he could possibly know and that God has a plan for the remainder of his life. Encourage him to have faith. Explain that his suffering can be offered up for his past sins and for the sins of others. Give some examples of how his seemingly meaningless suffering can actually help others. There are many stories of people whose families have drawn closer together when one of their relatives was dying. Or perhaps you could teach the person about the love Jesus displayed for us when he died on the Cross.

If the person does not have a relationship with God, first show the love of God through your example. You can then gently and lovingly ask if he would be open to hearing about how he can receive the free gift of eternal life. If he is a Catholic, consider asking a priest to administer the sacrament of the anointing of the sick and to offer counsel. Most priests have dealt with these situations many times. If he is not open to seeing a priest, you should compassionately tell him how God sent his only Son to reconcile the world to himself, and that Jesus truly wants to enter into his heart to forgive his sins. Gently encourage him to go to confession. Be sure to pray for guidance. If the person is unable to speak, just spend time with him, holding his hand and praying for him.

Question #92

"I've been debating with Protestants on the Internet for a while, and I'm feeling burned out. I get so wrapped up that I spend hours on end in arguments in chat rooms. I feel like my spiritual life is out of balance. What would you recommend?"

A. You are certainly not the first to have noble intentions and then end up feeling burned out. While it is great to share the Faith, it is remarkably easy to get sick of theological arguments. Why? In the words of St. Thérèse, "it is a much better thing to talk *to* God than to talk *about* God, since there is so much self-love intermingled with spiritual conversations." Sometimes, we read Scripture for the express purpose of trying to find verses to sling at someone else. That is not what it is for. St. Mark the Ascetic said, "A humble and spiritually active man, when he reads the Holy Scriptures, will refer everything to himself and not to another."

It is also important to remember that the salvation of others does not depend on you—it depends on God. In reality, it is the grace of Christ that changes hearts and convicts people to live in the truth of Christ and his Church. Remembering this when defending and explaining the Faith can help to "lower the stakes" in your mind and help keep you more balanced and less anxious in your approach to evangelization.

As Jesus said, "Martha, Martha, you are upset and anxious about many things. There is but one thing necessary" (Lk 10:41-42). That "one thing" Jesus is talking about is to know and love *him*. If you are feeling burnt out, it may be a good idea to ask our Lord for a greater love for him. Stand as a beggar before Jesus in the Holy Eucharist; stand before Mary and ask for a portion of her love for him. Give of yourself in works of charity in place of the time you are spending on the Internet.

Chapter 8

CATHOLIC BELIEFS
AND PRACTICES

Question #93

"My girlfriend says that baptism is just a symbol and does nothing to affect our souls. What does the Bible say about this?"

A. The belief that baptism does nothing to a person's soul and that no grace is given to the person is an idea that dates from the Protestant Reformation in the 1500s. For the previous fifteen centuries going all the way back to Jesus, all Christians unanimously agreed that one was "born again" through the saving words and water of baptism and that this sacrament brought about the remission of sin and entrance into God's family, the Church.

Here are some of the biblical verses that support the Catholic belief that baptism has real spiritual power and is much more than a mere symbol with no effect:

- At the end of St. Matthew's Gospel, we read that Jesus gave his apostles the command to "go therefore and make disciples of all nations, *baptizing* them in the name of the Father and of the Son and of the Holy Spirit, teaching them to observe all that I have commanded you" (Mt 28:19-20; emphasis added). It is difficult to imagine what he was talking about if baptism is unimportant or merely a symbol.

- In Acts 2:38, St. Paul teaches, "Repent, and be *baptized* every one of you, in the name of Jesus Christ for the forgiveness of your sins; and you shall receive the gift of the Holy Spirit" (emphasis added).

- At another point in Acts, St. Luke recounts that Ananias told Paul, "And now why do you wait? Rise and be *baptized*, and wash away your sins, calling on his name" (Acts 22:16; emphasis added).

- Because baptism gives us the Holy Spirit and washes away our sins, St. Peter said, "[In the Ark] a few, that is, eight persons, were saved through water. *Baptism*, which corresponds to this, *now saves you*" (1 Pt 3:20-21; emphasis added).

Both Peter and Paul have a concept of baptism that was formed by Christ himself, who taught, "Truly, truly, I say to you, unless one is born of water and the Spirit, he cannot enter the kingdom of God" (Jn 3:5). Later in the same chapter of John, we read: "After this, Jesus and his disciples went into the land of Judea … and *baptized*" (Jn 3:22; emphasis added). So we can see that baptism was central to the life and ministry of Jesus, and there is a solid biblical basis for seeing baptism as a truly cleansing sacrament with a powerful effect on our souls.

Question #94

"There is no basis in the Bible for baptizing infants. So why do some Christians—including Catholics—do this?"

A. Actually, there *is* a strong biblical basis for baptizing babies. Before presenting this evidence, though, we need to address an important issue.

Your question implies that if something is not explicitly taught in the Bible, then it should not be believed. This is a theory called *sola scriptura* ("Scripture alone"), and it was first taught by Martin Luther during the Protestant Reformation in the early sixteenth century. This belief forms the very foundation upon which Protestant Christianity is based. Ironically, though, belief in *sola scriptura* is not found anywhere in the Bible! In fact, the Bible actually commands us to hold fast to traditions that are not written down (see 2 Thess 2:15).

And remember, the very *canon* of Scripture (that is, the list of inspired books) cannot be found in the Bible. So how do we know that the seventy-three books (46 in the Old Testament, and 27 in the New Testament) contained in our Bible are divinely-inspired? We know this through the teaching authority of the Church, which determined the answer to this question at the Council of Hippo in AD 393. As we will see in a moment, this same Church baptized babies. We can, therefore, trust its authority in both matters.

Regarding infant baptism, the Bible speaks often about entire households being baptized, and the Greek word for household—*oikos*—would naturally include children. The notion that children should be denied baptism is a new phenomenon, about which the early Christians knew nothing at all. In fact, a dispute did arise among the early Christians regarding baptizing babies ... but the debate was over whether or not Christian parents had to wait eight days to baptize the infant. The very first Christians knew what Paul taught—that baptism replaced circumcision (Col 2:11-12). Under the Old Covenant, the child was circumcised eight days after birth and brought into a covenant relationship with God as an infant— thus joining the family of God, Israel. Under the New Covenant, baptism became the covenant sign of the new Israel, the Church. Baptism brings us, as infants, into the family of God.

Unfortunately, many Christians disagree about what baptism is and who should receive it. Baptists and Pentecostals don't baptize babies, but Lutherans and Methodists do. All four of these churches rely on the principle that the Bible is the sole rule of faith, yet they disagree about infant baptism, among many other things. So, how are we to know what the Bible means when it appears vague? We are to listen to the Church that Jesus established, because it is the "pillar and foundation of truth" (1 Tm 3:15).

Question #95

"If a person is not baptized, but lives a good life, can that person go to heaven?"

A. As Catholics, we affirm that baptism is necessary for salvation (see CCC 1257). In the Gospel of John, Jesus says clearly that unless one is born "of water and the Spirit, he cannot enter the kingdom of God" (Jn 3:5). We are born with a fallen nature due to original sin, and we enter the world without God's grace (see CCC 1250); we need to be "reborn" into this grace through baptism.

Naturally speaking, a "good life" is not sufficient to merit salvation. One reason for this is that "good" is often understood in a subjective way to be whatever each individual person believes.

This being said, as the *Catechism* states, "God has bound salvation to the sacrament of Baptism, but he himself is *not* bound by his sacraments" (CCC 1257; emphasis added). The Church has always held that a person who sincerely *desires* baptism, such as catechumens preparing to enter the Faith, can be saved (CCC 1259). This is called the *baptism of desire.*

Imagine that a person, through no fault of his own, has never been exposed to the saving teachings of Jesus. He or she can be saved if he or she strives to follow God's will *as he or she understands it.* As the Second Vatican Council teaches, salvation is possible for such people who, through no fault of their own, do not know the Gospel but follow their conscience and "strive to live a good life."[19]

One cannot be held responsible for what one genuinely doesn't know or understand. This is called *invincible ignorance,* which means that the person does not *choose* to be uniformed about the Faith. In this sense, there really may be some people who fall into this category because they live in remote regions of Africa or Asia—or even in the United States if they have been poorly catechized. However, with the spread of modern communications, it is becoming more unlikely that there are many places where the name of Jesus is not known. Ultimately, we must commend the soul of an unbaptized individual to the mercy of God. Only he knows the true state of a person's heart.

Question #96

"Where does the Bible say that the Church has the power to forgive sins?"

A. In John, chapter 20, Jesus comes to the apostles after rising from the dead. He tells them that just as the Father sent him, he is now sending the apostles out into the world. Keep in mind that Jesus was sent to reconcile the world to God and so took on the mission of bringing God's forgiveness to mankind. After saying this, Jesus *breathes* on the apostles and says, "Receive the Holy Spirit. If you forgive the sins of any, they are forgiven; if you retain the sins of any, they are retained" (Jn 20:22-23).

There are a few important things to point out here. For starters, this is one of only two places in the entire Bible where God "breathes" on anyone. The other is in Genesis when God breathed into Adam the "breath of life" (see Gn 2:7), so we can be sure that something monumental is taking place. In Genesis, God "breathes" life into man; in John's Gospel, Jesus "breathes" on his apostles the power to forgive sins, to restore supernatural life to the soul. Notice he didn't simply tell them to *announce* God's forgiveness to mankind—he actually gave them a share in his own authority to forgive people's sins.

It is also clear in Matthew 9:8 that the first Christians understood that the Church had authority to forgive sins. In this passage, when the crowds witnessed Jesus' power in forgiving sins, they were astounded and "they glorified God, who had given such authority to men." This implies that the power to forgive sins is shared by those to whom Jesus has passed on his own power—namely, the apostles.

Question #97

"Why do I have to go to a priest for confession? Why can't I go straight to God?"

A. First, we need to be clear: Only God can forgive sins (see CCC 1441; Mk 2:7). But Jesus, the God-Man, entrusted his apostles with a "ministry of reconciliation" (see 2 Cor 5:18) and, to accomplish this ministry, gave them the power to forgive sins (see CCC 1442). In John 20:21-23, Jesus tells the apostles that any sins they forgive are forgiven and any sins they retain are retained.

Why didn't Jesus just have his followers "confess" their sins directly to God in prayer? Why does he ask us to go to priest, another human being, to confess and receive absolution? Simply because our sins wound not only ourselves and our relationship with God; they harm our relationship with others and with the Church (see CCC 1443). Priests, by virtue of their ordination, have been given the power to forgive our sins and reconcile us to God and the Church. Although it must be said that not all priests are gifted with equal ability and wisdom in spiritual counseling, another part of their mission within the sacrament of reconciliation is to offer us encouragement and spiritual guidance. This spiritual direction can be very beneficial for growth, despite the discomfort we may feel in confessing our sins. We need to remember that humility is *good* for us!

Since Jesus has established a way for us to have our sins forgiven and to be restored to his grace, we should go to confession often. If we don't take advantage of this opportunity, we will be like the three-year-old who, while walking out of a store with his father, decides to run ahead to the car. "Let me pick you up," his father offers, but the boy keeps running: "No, Dad. I'm fast. Just watch me." Of course, the boy eventually gets to the car, but he would have gotten there twice as fast if he had let his dad carry him. Similarly, God hears us when we ask for forgiveness, but he wants us to be "carried" by our spiritual fathers on earth, the priests.

Remember: Jesus knows us better than we know ourselves. He knows what is best for us, and what truly brings us close to him. He gave us the sacrament of reconciliation because we need it.

Question #98

"If Jesus really died for the sins of the world once and for all, then why do we need confession? Doesn't confession take away from Jesus' sacrifice on the Cross?"

A. No, it doesn't. Confession does not add to or take away from the redemptive sacrifice of Jesus on the Cross; it actually demonstrates the power of the Cross.

As soon as he rose from the dead, Jesus appeared to the apostles and breathed on them, saying, "Receive the Holy Spirit. If you forgive the sins of any, they are forgiven; if you retain the sins of any, they are retained" (Jn 20:22-23; CCC 1441). Before breathing on the apostles, Jesus tells them that as the Father has sent him, so he sends them (see Jn 20:21). Something *huge* is happening here! Jesus is not simply commissioning them to preach; he is giving them the power to forgive sins.

Jesus gave his apostles authority over unclean spirits, authority to heal, and authority to raise people from the dead. Similarly, in Matthew 9:8, after Jesus had forgiven the sins of the paralytic and healed him, the Bible says that the crowd was astonished that God had given this authority to human beings. So, just as Jesus gave his disciples all these other forms of authority that do not take away from his work, but rather show it to us, so also is the confessional a sigzn of the Father's door—always open for the prodigal son to return home. It is a great gift and an outright proclamation of what Christ has done for the world.

Question #99

"How can I know what to confess and what not to confess?"

A. The Church teaches that every mortal sin must be confessed (see CCC 1456). If you are not sure if a particular sin is mortal or venial, ask your confessor (i.e., the priest hearing your confession) for guidance. In a sense, since you are already going to confession, it doesn't really matter whether the sin is mortal or not—it will be forgiven by the priest's words of absolution (if you repent of the sin and resolve not to do it again). This being said, the Church encourages us to confess every sin that we can recall committing, even if they are venial. As the *Catechism* says, "The regular confession of our venial sins helps us form our conscience, fight against evil tendencies, let ourselves be healed by Christ and progress in the life of the Spirit" (CCC 1458). Such humility is pleasing to God, and helps us gain the maximum benefit from the grace of the sacrament.

Before you go to confession, try spending at least ten minutes in prayer before the Blessed Sacrament. During this time, examine your conscience and see what sins are on your heart. Finally, ask God to enlighten your mind and show you your faults; it is only by being aware of our weaknesses that we can pray for help in the areas we need it most.

Question #100

"How do we know that Jesus was not speaking symbolically when he said, 'This is my body'?"

A. According to biblical scholars, there are more than three hundred different interpretations of the words, "This is my body." So, how are we to know for sure that the Catholic literal interpretation was held by the apostles? How do we know this was not a later belief?

As Catholics, we believe Jesus established the Church to teach in his name. In fact, the Bible is the book of the Church, and we can trust the interpretation given to these words by the very first Christians. In fact, we still have the writings from some of St. John's own disciples. These writings confirm that the early Church was unanimous in its understanding of the sixth chapter of John's Gospel—Jesus is truly present in the Eucharist. In fact, no one proposed that Jesus was speaking symbolically for more than one thousand years until Berengarius of Tours, who died in 1088, taught the heretical view that the Eucharist was merely symbolic.

When studying the words of the Last Supper, we need to remember that Jesus spoke Aramaic. In the Aramaic language, there are forty words or so that mean "represent" or "symbolize," but Jesus used none of them when speaking of the Eucharist. He literally said, "This is my body," and, "This is my blood" (see Mt 26:26-29; Mk 14:22-25; Lk 22:17-19).

In his first letter to the Corinthians, St. Paul said that whoever receives Communion unworthily is guilty of the

Body and the Blood of the Lord (see 1 Cor 11:27). In that culture, to be "guilty of another's body and blood" is to be guilty of murdering them. How could Paul say that someone was guilty of killing Jesus because he ate bread that symbolized him? Paul knew that the Eucharist was not merely a symbol but actually the Body, Blood, Soul, and Divinity of Jesus.

Question #101

"I don't feel any different when I receive the Eucharist. How do I know that it is helping my soul?"

A. The late Bishop Fulton Sheen, one of the greatest Catholic apologists and teachers of the twentieth century, told the story of a man who came up to him after a talk and said, "I have been going to daily Mass and receiving Communion every day for the past twenty-five years. I have to say that I don't think it has made any difference in my life. I still struggle with the same sins I always have." To this, Bishop Sheen responded, "Well, think how much *worse* you would be without the Eucharist!"

A good way to see the effects of someone else upon your life is to study your actions and reactions when that person is gone. For example, a young man once said that his life was influenced most by his grandfather—*after* his grandfather's death. It wasn't that he was influenced by the actual death. Rather, after his grandfather died, he better appreciated the things he had learned while his grandfather was alive. He also better recognized certain qualities and characteristics about himself that only existed because of his grandfather's influence. This can be similar to the way that Christ changes us within Mass and through our reception of the Eucharist. We may not feel a thing, but being in Christ's presence on a regular basis and regularly consuming the almighty and perfect God under the form of bread surely will change you. You may not recognize the effects of Eucharistic grace until later, when you react in certain situations more peacefully than before or realize it is a bit easier for you to forgive someone for a wrong they have done.

When we receive Communion, we are literally receiving the Body and Blood of Jesus; we are united with him in the most profound and intimate way possible (see CCC 1391). As Jesus said, "He who eats my flesh and drinks my blood abides in me, and I in him" (Jn 6:56). If Jesus "abides" (i.e., dwells) within us, then we will naturally be transformed and strengthened spiritually. Receiving the Eucharist cleanses us from past sins and helps preserve us from committing sins in the future (see CCC 1393, 1395). Of course, this does not mean that some of the particular sins and weaknesses we struggle with will instantly go away. But we can be sure that Christ's presence in the Eucharist will help us overcome them if we persevere.

Question #102

"Can I receive the Eucharist if I think I committed a mortal sin and plan to go to confession in the next few days?"

A. Ordinarily, no. We must be properly prepared to receive the Holy Eucharist; we must be in the state of God's grace. If you are conscious of having committed a mortal sin, you need to go to confession before receiving the Body and Blood of Jesus (see CCC 1385). St. Paul, in his first letter to the Corinthians, tells us that we need to examine our consciences before approaching this great sacrament: "Whoever, therefore, eats the bread or drinks the cup of the Lord in an unworthy manner will be guilty of profaning the body and blood of the Lord ... [he] eats and drinks judgment upon himself" (1 Cor 11:27-29). Here's a simple rule: If you are in doubt about whether or not you are in the state of grace, don't receive Communion. Go to confession as soon as possible, and then receive in good conscience. If, however, you would cause scandal to others by not going to Communion, you could receive the Eucharist provided you make an act of contrition and resolve to go to confession as soon as possible.

Question #103

"Is it a serious sin to miss Sunday Mass?"

A. Missing Mass on Sunday is a serious matter (see CCC 2042), but this does not mean it is always a mortal sin. For a sin to be mortal, three conditions must be met: (1) it must be a serious (i.e., grave) matter; (2) one must have full knowledge of the action he or she is doing (or not doing), and (3) one must fully consent to the action— he or she must freely choose it of his or her own will. If any of these aspects is lacking, the sin is merely venial.

Sometimes, circumstances beyond our control prevent us from attending Mass on Sunday. For example, if your car breaks down on your way to church, you certainly do not *intend* to miss Mass—so there is no free consent of your will. In such a case, no sin at all would be committed. Similarly, if you are seriously ill, you are not required to pull yourself out of bed and drag yourself to Mass, especially if you sincerely desire to go. Also, if you absolutely need to travel over a weekend (e.g., on a fourteen-hour flight to Australia) and cannot go to Mass, although you sincerely want to, this, too, would not be sinful.

It's a different story, though, if you can get to Mass and you know that missing it is a serious sin, but you deliberately lay around on the couch anyway watching TV. Such behavior would objectively meet the requirements of a mortal sin. But only God can be the judge of this because only he knows if you have full knowledge and consent of the will. In a certain sense, though, God is *not* the only one who can figure out if this is a mortal sin. Once you understand the conditions of mortal sin, you should generally be able to figure out what is and is not a mortal sin in your own life! You should know what went on inside your conscience before the action and be able to honestly admit to yourself and to God whether or not you freely chose to do something that you fully understood was seriously wrong. In short, deliberately missing Sunday Mass is objectively a serious matter, but it's only a mortal sin if one fully knows this and consents to this action.

Question #104

"Why do Catholics have to go to church on Sunday instead of any day of the week that one may want to go?"

A. Simply because Sunday is the day we celebrate the Lord's resurrection from the dead. The third commandment states: "Remember the Sabbath day, to keep it holy" (Ex 20:8; Dt 5:12). For the Jewish people, the Sabbath falls on the seventh day of the week, Saturday, the day God rested from Creation. The Christian church has always, since the days of the apostles, celebrated the Eucharist on Sunday as a way of commemorating Jesus' resurrection (see CCC 2177–2179).

Question #105

"My Protestant friend says that kneeling before a 'piece of bread' during Eucharistic Adoration is idolatry. How should I answer him?"

A. If the sacred host we kneel before in Eucharistic Adoration were just a "piece of bread," then your friend would be correct—it would be idolatry. It would be no different from praying to a golden calf or a statue. But, if what appears to be a piece of bread is actually the Body of Christ, then we are kneeling before God himself.

In the Old Testament, there were several occasions when an angel took on human form to carry out the work of God. Even though the angel looked like a human being, it remained an angel. If an angel can, by the power of God, take on human appearance, Jesus is infinitely able to humble himself under the appearance of bread in order that we might receive him in the Eucharist.

Question #106

"In addition to renewing our baptismal vows, what does confirmation do for us spiritually?"

A. Along with baptism and Eucharist, confirmation is one of the sacraments of "initiation." While baptism washes away original sin and brings us into communion with the Church, confirmation more perfectly joins us to God's people and gives us a "special grace of the Holy Spirit."

The *Catechism* says that the sacrament of confirmation "brings an increase and deepening of baptismal grace" and mentions some of the effects confirmation has in the life of the believer (see CCC 1303). Among other things, confirmation:

- Unites us more strongly to Jesus

- Increases the gifts of the Holy Spirit

- Gives us a special strength to spread the Faith

- Helps us live our faith more fruitfully and faithfully

We receive confirmation only once because, like baptism, it imprints a permanent "mark" on our souls (see CCC 1317). This means our souls are forever changed by this sacrament; we have been "sealed" by the Holy Spirit to be faithful disciples of Christ (see CCC 1304).

Question #107

"My non-Catholic friend asked me to show him where the sacrament of confirmation is in the Bible. How can I respond?"

A. References to confirmation are found throughout the Old and New Testaments. While the actual word *confirmation* (which literally means a "strengthening" or "to make firm") is not used, the reality it expresses can clearly be seen. Here are a few examples:

In the Old Testament, the prophet Isaiah announced that the "Spirit of the LORD" would rest upon the coming Messiah (see Is 11:2, 61:1). This prophecy was fulfilled when the Holy Spirit descended upon Jesus in the form of a dove during his baptism by John (see Mt 3:13-17). Jesus' entire life and ministry were carried out in "total communion with the Holy Spirit" (CCC 1286). In John's Gospel, we read how Jesus is given the Spirit "without measure" (Jn 3:34).

Jesus intended for his followers to share in this "fullness of the Spirit" which he himself possessed. Throughout the New Testament, Jesus promised an outpouring of the Spirit on his disciples (see Lk 12:12; Jn 3:5-8, 16:7-15; Acts 1:8), and these promises were fulfilled on the day of Pentecost: "Suddenly a sound came from heaven like the rush of a mighty wind, and it filled the house where they [the apostles] were sitting. And there appeared to them tongues as of fire, distributed and resting on each one of them. And they were filled with the Holy Spirit" (Acts 2:2-4). Now filled with the Spirit, the apostles began to preach the gospel without fear. Likewise, when we are confirmed, we are strengthened to be faithful followers of Jesus through the power of the Holy Spirit.

There are also other places in the New Testament where we can see the roots of confirmation as we know it today in the practices of the early Church. One example is when Paul laid his hands on some men and "the Holy Spirit came upon them" (Acts 19:6). Earlier in Acts, Peter and John laid hands on men that had already been baptized, and they also received the Holy Spirit (see Acts 8:16-17).

Question #108

"Is it right for my parents to force me to be confirmed?"

A. This is a tricky question. As we have said in a previous answer, until you are eighteen (or until you move out of the family home), you must respect and obey your parents, as long as what they are asking you to do is not sinful. One of the primary and God-given responsibilities parents have is to provide for the spiritual formation of their children. As faithful parents, they are called to ensure that their children are being raised in the Catholic Faith in the way the Church requires. So, even if you are sixteen or seventeen and think you are old enough to make your own decisions, your parents are right to "force" you to attend Mass on Sundays. They know that Sunday Mass is a vital part of your having a good relationship with God.

Your question, though, asks if your parents can *force* you to be confirmed. Strictly speaking, sacraments must be received freely and with a sincere desire to receive them. For example, no one can be forced to go to confession—in fact, such a confession would be a sacrilege and the absolution invalid because one must have true sorrow for their sins in order to have them forgiven. Nonetheless, your parents are well within their rights to "force" you to attend confirmation preparation classes because they are legitimately concerned with your spiritual well-being. Actually forcing you down the aisle of a church to be confirmed is another matter, though.

The sacrament of confirmation does require that the candidate must "have the intention of receiving the sacrament" (CCC 1319). This means that to receive the sacrament, you need to *want* to be confirmed. This is also why we wait to celebrate this sacrament until you reach the age of *reason*. This wait is not exercised so that you have more time to pick a cool confirmation name. Rather, the Church wants you to use your gifts of reason and free will to choose Christ and his Catholic Church for yourself.

Often, when Catholic teens struggle with making this choice, it quickly turns into a fight between them and their parents. If there ever were a proper "fight" (really, we mean a respectful debate) to be had between a teen and his or her parents, this is it. Why? Because this is when you choose for yourself what your parents chose for you at baptism. This is a big deal—a really big deal. If you don't want to be confirmed, you had better have some very good reasons. And your parents deserve to know what your reservations are and why. On the flip side, you need to understand why your parents so badly want you to be confirmed. Ask them to explain their reasons and try to see their point of view.

However, instead of arguing every night at dinner about it, you should use this time to *learn* and deeply *investigate* your Catholic Faith. If you cannot articulate solid reasons not to be confirmed, your parents will feel that your decision is not reasonable and thought-out. Instead, they will feel like you are dropping your faith and rebelling against them. If, after much respectful discussion, you can show them that you are still really trying to figure things out, then maybe they will agree to allow you to wait another year before making your decision to be confirmed. During that year, you could read more, study more, pray more, and truly try to better understand the Catholic Faith that your parents so desire you to choose for yourself.

If you are resisting being confirmed and resent your parents for wanting you to receive this sacrament, we would suggest you ask yourself the following questions: "If my Catholic faith means anything to me, why *don't* I want to be confirmed? Does my faith really matter? If not, *why* not?" You need to come up with some good answers to these questions; your parents and your Church have a right to know your true thoughts and feelings on the matter.

Question #109

"Why does the Church teach that there is no marriage in heaven?"

A. Because Jesus himself says as much. In Matthew 22:22-33, Jesus is debating the Sadducees on the question of the resurrection from the dead. They challenge him with a hypothetical situation about a woman who eventually married seven brothers in succession after each husband had died. The Sadducees wanted to know whose wife she would be in the resurrection, since she had been married to all seven men. Jesus, in a very clear statement on both the nature of marriage and on the reality of heaven, responds to them, saying, "You are wrong, because you know neither the Scriptures nor the power of God. For in the resurrection [people] neither marry nor are given in marriage, but are like angels in heaven" (Mt 22:29-30). So it is clear that marriage is for this life only. But why is this?

Marriage, as the *Catechism* teaches, "is by its nature ordered to the good of the spouses and the procreation and education of [children]" (CCC 1601). In other words, the purpose of marriage is to help husbands and wives grow in holiness, bring new life into the world, and ultimately bring the entire family to salvation in Christ. Marriage, then, is a means of getting to heaven. Also, marriage is an image—a foreshadowing—of the final heavenly marriage feast between Jesus, the Bridegroom, and the Church, his bride (see Rv 19:7; CCC 1602). It is a sign of things to come. Once we are in heaven, there is no need for marriage because we will have achieved our eternal destiny—union with God.

Question #110

"I'm hesitant to get married because my parents (and so many of my friends' parents) are divorced. What should I do?"

A. First, if you are a teenager, then you don't need to worry about getting married yet! What teens need to focus on is discerning their vocations—figuring out what God wants for your life: marriage, religious life, or Christian celibacy. If, in the future, you have discerned that God wants you to be married, then there is nothing to fear. If God wants it for your life, then it is the best thing for you.

Understandably, many people are nervous about following in the footsteps of their parents whose marriages failed. If your parents didn't set a great example for you, then you really need to find some other married couples who are enjoying good faith lives and healthy marriages. Find ways to spend some time with them, talk to them, and learn from them. They are bound to surprise you with their interesting stories! Many couples who have solid marriages really love to share their wisdom with others because they want others to experience the joy, peace, and love that they do. If you don't know any couples that want to share with you, you may want to go to your parish office; the pastor (or even the parish secretary) should be able to introduce you to those people you need to meet.

In the future, if you eventually find a special person whom you may spend the rest of your life loving, you should be up front about your questions and your fears and journey with that person in learning about what Christ wants for spouses in marriage.

In the meantime, pray hard, stay faithful to the sacraments, pay attention to all the relationships around you, and read as much good literature on Catholic marriage as you can find. Reading the section in the *Catechism* on marriage (CCC 1601–1666) and studying St. John Paul II's Theology of the Body should raise many questions and provide answers that will help you learn more about how a good, faithful, and faith-filled Catholic marriage works. And remember that God has great plans for your life, just as he reminds us, "For I know well the plans I have in mind for you, says the LORD … plans to give you a future and a hope" (Jer 29:11).

Question #111

"After a Catholic couple gets married in the Church can they ever re-marry?"

A. If one spouse dies, then the short answer to your question is "yes." If both spouses are alive, the short answer to your question is "no." The Church always presumes that a marriage between two Catholics before a priest is valid, and a valid marriage is, by its very nature, *indissoluble*—meaning that no human authority, even the Church, can dissolve the marital bond that has been created (see CCC 1614, 1615). This being said, what may have appeared to be a valid marriage is sometimes proven otherwise during the process of an annulment (CCC 1629).

An *annulment* (officially known as a "decree of nullity"), contrary to popular opinion, is *not* a "Catholic divorce." It is merely the official declaration of a Church tribunal that a particular marriage is not—and never was—valid. In other words, though the couple went through a wedding ceremony, they were never truly married in the eyes of

God and the Church. This is because one of the three necessary components of marriage was missing (or defective) at the time of the wedding. These components are *consent, form,* and *capacity.* Here's what each of these means:

- *Consent*—this is the most important component because it literally "makes the marriage," as the *Catechism* puts it (see CCC 1626); this consists of the exchange of vows, by which "the partners mutually give themselves to each other" (CCC 1627); this must be a completely free act on the part of both spouses, free from fear or coercion (see CCC 1627). So-called "shotgun" weddings, in which the couple is forced to get married by an angry father, would be invalid. Most annulments are granted because of a defect in the consent of one or both spouses.

- *Form*—this refers to the requirement that Catholics must follow the *canonical form* of the Church when they get married. In other words, they must follow the Church's laws on marriage. These require that Catholics get married in a Catholic church in the presence of an ordained minister of the Church, either a priest or deacon (see CCC 1631). If a Catholic wants to get married outside of the Church, he or she must be granted a *dispensation from form* by his or her local bishop. If they go ahead and get married without this dispensation, the marriage would normally be considered invalid. (By the way, only Catholics are bound by canonical form.)

- *Capacity*—both spouses must have the *capacity* (that is, the ability) to get married. For example, they must have reached a certain minimum age; they must not have an *impediment* to marriage, such as religious vows or priestly ordination; they must be able to consummate the marriage through sexual intercourse, at least once (men who are permanently impotent cannot validly marry); they must be able to give consent (some mentally disabled persons may not be able to get married because they do not understand what marriage requires). Usually, pastors will determine whether or not a couple has the capacity for marriage long before the wedding is even scheduled. As a result, annulments are rarely granted for defects in capacity.

If a couple is granted an annulment, then they are free to "re-marry." But, technically speaking, "re-marry" is not the right word to use because they never were truly married in first place. They are simply "getting married."

Question #112

"Did the Church invent the idea of annulments or does it come from the Bible?"

A. First of all, the Church doesn't "invent" any of its doctrines—it merely passes on what has been revealed by Jesus and handed on by the apostles. Secondly, as we have mentioned in a previous answer, not all of the Church's teachings and practices are explicitly found in the Bible (nor do they need to be). This is because God's revelation to us consists of both the Bible and Sacred Tradition. It is the role of the teaching authority of the Church (that is, the pope and the bishops united with him), guided by the Holy Spirit, to interpret the contents of this revelation and make definitive judgments for the people of God.

While the actual process of annulments is part of the disciplinary law of the Church (which Christ did give the Church the authority to legislate; see Mt 18:18), the "idea" of annulments is rooted in the very nature of marriage itself, which is *clearly* mentioned in the Bible. As we have said in the previous answer, in order for a couple to be validly married, they must give valid consent, follow the proper form for marriage, and have the capacity for marriage. If any of these three components is lacking, then a marriage never truly existed. So an annulment does not change reality; it does not make a couple who was married suddenly "unmarried." An annulment merely *declares* that something that was thought to exist—a marriage—in actuality does not.

Question #113

"I have family members who say that a marriage by a justice of the peace is valid in the eyes of God. What would the Church say?"

A. It depends on *who* is getting married. If we are talking about two non-Catholics getting married, then a marriage before a justice of the peace would be considered valid in the eyes of God. If, however, one or both of the spouses is Catholic, then the marriage would not be valid. Why is this?

Well, we first need to mention a couple of things about the nature of marriage. Marriage is a lifelong covenant between a man and a woman in which they bind themselves exclusively to each other for their own good and the good of any children with which God may bless them. In the Roman Catholic view, it is through the exchange of vows that this covenant is ratified and the marriage actually takes place (see CCC 1623).

For a Catholic, the exchange of vows must normally be in the presence of an ordained minister of the Church (either a priest or, in some dioceses, a deacon)—in other words, Catholics are required to observe the proper *form* of marriage prescribed by the Church. Otherwise, their marriage could be considered invalid. While it is possible to receive a special permission (called a *dispensation*) from form, this would normally be to permit a Catholic to get married in a non-Catholic Christian church, not in front of a justice of the peace. Since non-Catholics are not bound by Catholic form, they are able to validly marry in almost any setting; the only necessary element would be that they exchange vows before a witness and that they intend marriage to be for life.

Question #114

"If a Catholic wants to marry a non-Christian, could the couple get married in the Church?"

A. Marrying a non-Christian in the Church is more difficult than marrying a Protestant Christian, but it can be done. This is because the Church is aware of the difficulties that will be faced by the couple due to their different faiths and wants to make sure that the couple is making a prudent decision to get married. In addition to the same norms or laws established for marrying a Protestant, as mentioned in the last answer, the couple must also get a dispensation from the bishop. Failure to do this makes the marriage invalid.

Question #115

"What is the Church's view on interracial marriages?"

A. It has no problem with them whatsoever. The color of one's skin has no bearing on an individual's ability to marry anyone, regardless of race. You may sometimes hear of the Church referring to "mixed marriages." In this case, though, the Church means the marriage of a Catholic with a non-Catholic, not an interracial marriage.

Some pastors or counselors may offer additional marriage preparation to engaged couples of different races to help them overcome some challenges they may experience as a result of their union. Even though our society has come a long way towards racial equality and acceptance, there are still some people who have difficulty accepting interracial couples. Sometimes these people are even members of the couple's own families.

The important thing in any marriage is whether the two people are socially and spiritually compatible. If one of the spouses ends up in hell because they were not spiritually challenged or supported by the other, then that marriage can be considered a failure to a great extent. If the children go to hell, partly because of their parents' difficulties in coming together in religious matters, this marriage should also be considered a failure to a great extent. (*Note:* As we have said elsewhere in this book, no one can *make* another person go to hell. By their own actions, an individual ultimately decides where he or she will spend eternity. But influences from others—particularly one's spouse—can greatly contribute to a person's spiritual attitude and, ultimately, his or her eternal fate.)

When choosing a marriage partner, the first question one should ask is: *Will this person help me and our future children be holy and be saved?* Things like romantic love, physical attraction, intelligence, sense of humor, etc., are also important, but they are not as important as *spiritual*

compatibility. For this, we must pray to God that he will
lead us to choose the person he intends for us.

Question #116

"Can a married Catholic man become a priest after his wife dies?"

A. Yes, he can, provided he meets the other requirements
necessary for admission to the seminary. In fact, many
dioceses and religious orders are especially interested in
older vocations because of the maturity level and wisdom
that these men often bring to the priesthood. Their life
experience often makes them able to relate to the concerns
of lay people in a very fruitful way.

Question #117

"If a priest gets married, can he continue being a priest?"

A. No. A Catholic priest who "leaves the priesthood" to
marry must first be released from his priestly obligations
by the competent authorities in the Vatican. Therefore, he
would not be permitted to function as a priest following
his marriage. Of course, he would still have the priestly
powers to forgive sins and consecrate the Eucharist, but
he would be forbidden to use them except in extreme
emergencies (i.e., if someone were dying and no other
priest was available).

Most men who leave the priesthood seek a *dispensation*
from their ordination promises of celibacy and obedience
(or, if they are a member of a religious order, their vows
of poverty, chastity, and obedience). This process is
commonly called *laicization,* which removes a priest from
the clerical state. Strictly speaking, though, laicization does

not really transform a priest into a layperson, because the sacrament of holy orders imprints an indelible mark on his soul; he is a priest for all eternity.

Question #118

"My Protestant friend says we shouldn't call priests 'father.' Didn't Jesus tell us to 'call no man your father' in Matthew 23:9?"

A. The passage you mention, Matthew 23:9, like all other verses of the Bible, must be read in its proper context. If you look through the New Testament, you will find at least 140 instances of various people—Jewish patriarchs, Christian leaders, or biological fathers—being referred to as "father." It is clear, then, that when Jesus commanded us to call no man on earth "father," he was not speaking literally. Otherwise, it would be sinful to refer to the man married to your mother as "father." In the context of his teaching, Jesus was simply telling his disciples to put no human being on the level of God, our heavenly Father.

St. Paul says, "For though you have countless guides to Christ, you do not have many *fathers*. For I became your *father* in Christ Jesus through the gospel" (1 Cor 4:14-15; emphasis added). In response to the high priest, St. Stephen said, "Brethren and *fathers,* hear me. The God of glory appeared to our *father* Abraham" (Acts 7:2; emphasis added). There is nothing wrong with the word "father," provided we do not place another person at the same level of the heavenly Father. The reason why earthly men are given the name "father" is precisely to remind us of God's fatherly love. It is the same with our Catholic priests. We call them "fathers" because they are spiritual leaders—our fathers in faith—who, by their total commitment to Christ and the

Church, become earthly images of God's total commitment to love and provide for us.

Question #119

"Why do priests wear black?"

A. In North America and western Europe, priests wear black to show that they are "dead to the world" in order to be alive for Christ and service to his Church. Traditionally, priests wore a *cassock*—a long, ankle-length robe— around the parish church. Today, most priests wear a clerical shirt with a Roman collar and black pants. In warmer climates, though, some priests actually wear lighter colors, usually white.

Question #120

"How old do you have to be in order to become a priest or nun?"

A. According to the *Code of Canon Law,* the Church's official collection of ecclesiastical laws, a man must be at least twenty-five years old to be ordained.[20] There is no maximum age limit to be ordained, though some dioceses will not accept a man to the seminary if he is past a certain age, typically forty-five or fifty. This is because the extended period of time that seminary training requires (typically five to eight years) often puts these men close to retirement by the time they finish seminary.

Regarding nuns, the minimum age that a woman will be accepted varies depending on the religious order. Few orders accept those under the age of eighteen, and nearly all require the woman to graduate from high school first. In addition, canon law states that a candidate for religious life must be at least seventeen before being admitted to the novitiate, the start of the official training for religious life.[21]

Question #121

"Why are girls allowed to be altar servers but women are not allowed to be priests?"

A. First, we need to realize that the ministry of altar servers was not established by Jesus; it was established by the Church to assist priests as they celebrate Mass. As such, the rules governing who can be an altar server and what their proper role should be are entirely *ecclesiastical*, that is, determined by the Church. This means they can be changed as needed. Traditionally, only boys assisted at the altar; this was seen as a way of encouraging vocations to the priesthood. More recently, the Church has determined that girls could serve as effectively as boys, and many are doing an outstanding job.

But the priesthood is a completely different matter. It is not of merely ecclesiastical origin; the priesthood comes from Jesus himself. It was he who chose his apostles and gave them a share in his ministry, telling them to teach all nations (see Mt 28:18-20). Significantly, Jesus chose only men to be his apostles. There are rich theological reasons for this, none of which have anything to do with sexism or the oppression of women, as some today claim.

You may hear some people who advocate the ordination of women to the priesthood say that Jesus chose only men as apostles because he was bound by the cultural norms of his times. But Jesus broke with nearly every major cultural norm his Jewish contemporaries held dear—for a rabbi to even speak to a woman was unheard of in his day, but Jesus had many women among his followers; he performed miracles on the Sabbath; he ate in the homes of known sinners and tax collectors; he defied the religious authorities of his day, calling them "whitewashed tombs" and "hypocrites"; he kicked the moneychangers out of the Temple; and he openly referred to himself as the Son of God. In fact, it was Jesus' *disregard* for societal norms that got him into trouble with the Jewish and Roman authorities, ultimately leading to his crucifixion. If Jesus had wanted to choose women to be among his apostles, he certainly would have done so, especially given that nearly every major religion of his day (with the important exception of Judaism) had priestesses.

We need to remember that women played a key role in spreading the gospel. In fact, they were the first to tell the news of the risen Christ. If Jesus had wanted women to be priests, he would have had the ideal candidate in his Mother Mary. But even she was not among the apostles. As St. Paul points out in his first letter to the Corinthians, each of us are called to use the particular gifts we have been given for the good of the Church. He writes, "Now there are varieties of gifts, but the same Spirit; and there are varieties of service, but the same Lord; and there are varieties of working, but it is the same God who inspires them all ..." (1 Cor 12:4-6). Later, Paul continues, saying, "you are the body of Christ and individually members of it. And God has appointed in the Church first apostles, second prophets, third teachers, then workers of miracles, the healers, then administrators ... are all apostles? Are all prophets? Are all teachers? Do all work miracles?" (1 Cor 12:27-29). This was to indicate that all of us play different roles in the Church.

Think of it this way: Women bring members of Christ's "body" (i.e., the Church) into the world every time

‹›8

they give birth. Men do not have this ability, which is a great privilege. Priests bring the Body of Christ—the Holy Eucharist—into the world one Mass at a time—a gift reserved to them, acting *in persona Christi* (in the person of Christ).

St. John Paul II officially stated that "the Church has no authority whatsoever to confer priestly ordination on women and that this judgment is to be definitively held by all the Church's faithful."[22] With these words, the Holy Father is simply confirming what the Church has always taught. In fact, he definitively settled the issue by indicating that the ordination of women is no longer a subject that is open for debate among Catholics.

Question #122
"Where is anointing of the sick in the Bible?"

A. In James 5:14-15, we read: "Are any among you sick? Let him call for the elders of the church, and let them pray over him, anointing him with oil in the name of the Lord; and the prayer of faith will save the sick man, and the Lord will raise him up; and if he has committed sins, he will be forgiven." Also, in the Gospel of Mark, the apostles go out and preach the gospel, drive out demons, and anoint sick people with oil (see Mk 6:12-13). Anointing of the sick is a healing, sacramental part of the whole package of bringing the gospel to the world. These passages are as clear as it gets when looking for biblical support for the Catholic belief in the sacrament of the anointing of the sick.

Question #123

"Can agnostics go to heaven?"

A. For those of you who are not familiar with the term, an *agnostic* is someone who questions whether God exists or whether it is even possible to know if he exists at all. (An *atheist,* on the other hand, absolutely denies God's existence.) This skeptical belief system, however, does not always mean that the person is living an immoral life. Some may be good people who genuinely care about the well-being of others. There are many agnostics who are sincerely seeking the truth; they just have not yet discovered it in the Catholic Faith.

While it is true that there is no salvation apart from Jesus Christ, the sole Messiah and Savior of the world, this does not mean that explicit belief in Jesus is absolutely required to be saved. Someone who is incapable of making an explicit act of faith in Jesus (e.g., the mentally disabled) can still be saved if he or she follows God's will as he or she understands it. In God's merciful love, such people may still be saved through Christ via an application of the graces he earned on the Cross.

This chance at salvation also applies to those who, through no fault of their own, do not know of Jesus or his Church, but who live in accordance with the graces God gives to them. The German theologian, Karl Rahner (1904–1984), coined a term—"the anonymous Christian"— which is often used in reference to these people who live lives of virtue and goodness without actually knowing Jesus Christ. In such a case, though, the person is still saved through the saving work of Jesus on the Cross.

God, being just, gives all people an opportunity for salvation since he "wills all men to be saved" (1 Tm 2:4). St. Peter added, "God shows no partiality. Rather, in every nation whoever fears him and acts uprightly is acceptable to him" (Acts 10:35). St. Paul mentioned that the law of God has been written on all hearts, and therefore, men know God (Rom 1:21), even if no Mosaic Law has been given to them. Men will be judged based on what they *knew*—and how they lived their lives as a result of this knowledge. Some Jews could be damned, and some Gentiles saved if they observed the prescriptions of the law "by nature" (Rom 2:14). As Paul tells the Romans, "There is no partiality with God. All who sin outside the law will also perish without reference to it" (Rom 2:11-12).

By the same principle of God's judgment, the Church does not propose to know if any particular soul is damned. Only God can judge the heart.

Question #124

"I read in a pamphlet that one simply has to profess Jesus as one's 'personal Lord and Savior' to be saved. This seems too easy. What is the Catholic view of how one gets to heaven?"

A. You're right—it *does* seem too easy. In fact, much more is required. Actually, your parents professed Jesus as your Savior when you were baptized, and then you make your own profession when you are confirmed. Every time you attend Mass, you are professing Jesus as your Savior: you say the Nicene Creed and respond "Amen" before receiving the Eucharist. It is true that faith in Jesus is the means of our salvation, but this is more than just a once-and-done, singular act—it involves a lifetime of living in his grace and striving to do his will in our lives.

Among other things, the Bible says that to be saved we should be baptized (Jn 3:3-5), keep the commandments (see Mt 19:17; 1 Jn 3:19-24, 5:3), do the will of God the Father (see Mt 7:21), do good works with faith and love (see Gal 5:6; Jas 1:22, 2:24), and believe—have real faith—in Jesus (see Lk 7:50; Eph 2:8). As you can see, the Bible actually says there are many things we must do in order to get to heaven, *including* professing our faith in Christ with our mouths (Rom 10:9-11).

Question #125

"What does it mean to be 'born again'? I hear this phrase often but don't know what it means."

A. When you hear some Christians use the expression "born again," they are describing a particular moment in their lives when they had a radical conversion to Jesus, the moment when they "became a Christian" and experienced a desire to do God's will in their lives. For many evangelical Christians, this experience was so powerful that they can actually remember the exact date when it happened. They may say something like, "I gave my heart to the Lord," or, "I became a Christian," or, "I got saved on July 6, 1993." This sounds strange to Catholic ears, because we believe we were committed to Christ the day we were baptized. Nonetheless, many Catholics also have similar and powerful conversion experiences when they go from being lukewarm in their faith to being on fire for Jesus.

When you encounter a "born again" Christian, he or she will usually ask you one of the following questions: "Are you saved?" or "Do you know Jesus as your personal Lord and Savior? or "Are you a Christian?" As a faithful Catholic, you can truly answer "yes" to all these questions. You can then go on to explain that salvation is not a once-and-done event, but a lifelong process. You can then say something like this: "I *was* saved and became a Christian on the day of my baptism. As I pray and do his will every day, I *am* being saved. If I persevere in God's grace until death, I *will* be saved and spend eternity with God in heaven." So salvation is a *past, present,* and *future* reality.

Question #126

"I went to a Bible camp with a friend and they taught that once you are saved, nothing can undo that. Is it possible for a Christian to lose salvation?"

A. The idea of "once saved, always saved" was first proposed by John Calvin during the Protestant Reformation in the sixteenth century. Among many evangelical and fundamentalist Christians today, this belief is known as the doctrine of "eternal security." Prior to Calvin, all Christians believed that one was free to walk away from God through mortal sin. The Scriptures give several examples of people falling away from the Faith. Here are some of the clearest passages:

1. In John 15, Jesus says that he is the vine, and we are the branches. "If you keep my commandments, you will remain in my love" (15:10). However, four verses earlier, he says, "Anyone who does not remain in me will be thrown out like a branch and wither; people will gather them and throw them into a fire and they will be burned" (15:6). This does not sound like "once saved, always saved," since Jesus speaks of some people being taken off the vine if they do not keep his commandments.

2. John continues this theme in his first letter, when he says, "there is such a thing as deadly sin ... all wrongdoing is sin, but there is sin that is not deadly" (1 Jn 5:16-17). If the sin is "deadly" (that is, *mortal*), then this clearly indicates that we may choose to "kill ourselves" spiritually and, if we persist in this sin, die in a state of separation from God.

3. In his letter to the Romans, St. Paul speaks about the "obedience of faith" (Rom 1:5, 16:26). He also says in his letter to the Galatians that some have been "separated from Christ" and have "fallen from grace" (Gal 5:4).

4. St. Paul advises the Philippians to work out their salvation in "fear and trembling" (Phil 2:12). If losing salvation was a "done deal," there would be no reason to write this—instead, St. Paul might have written something like, "Congratulations, Philippians, on getting saved. I'm happy for you and look forward to seeing you all in heaven."

5. Now it seems clear that you can't "fall from grace" unless you were once in grace, and you can't be separated from Jesus, unless you were once united to him. St. Paul stresses this reality several times, exhorting the Corinthians to avoid immorality, telling the Christian community there that fornicators, drunkards, etc., will not enter the kingdom of God (see 1 Cor 6:9-10). (Remember, St. Paul wrote his letters to believers.)

6. St. Paul is perhaps most blunt in Romans 11:22, when he says, "See then, the kindness and severity of God; severity towards those who fell, but God's kindness to you, provided you remain in his

kindness. Otherwise you too will be cut off." Paul even extends this same warning to himself, when he says that we should guard against overconfidence (1 Cor 9:27–10:12).

All of these warnings should not lead us to fear, since God is always faithful and will always help us to avoid sin (1 Cor 10:13). Our job is to continually say "yes" to him by striving always to do his will. This involves being obedient to his Church and its teachings, and by listening to Jesus as he leads us in our prayers.

Question #127

"What happens after we die?"

A. As the *Catechism* says, "Death puts an end to human life as the time open to either accepting or rejecting the divine grace manifested in Christ" (CCC 1021). In other words, there are no more opportunities to grow in holiness; there are no second chances. After we die, we immediately stand before the judgment seat of Jesus, and he will reward us based on how we have lived our lives, on how we have responded to the blessings and graces he gave us. This is called the *particular* judgment, because it refers to each person individually. If we have died in the state of grace, we will go to heaven, either directly or after spending some time in purgatory. If we have died in a state of mortal sin, we will go immediately to hell (see CCC 1022).

Many in our culture are afraid of death. Why? Probably because they do not really grasp the meaning of *life*. As St. John of the Cross so eloquently puts it, "At the evening of life, we shall be judged on our love" (see CCC 1022).[23] We need to prepare ourselves for death by living our lives as Jesus calls us to—by loving him with all our strength and loving our neighbors as ourselves. Many of the great saints longed for their time on earth to come to an end so that they could go home to be with the Lord. They were unafraid of death because they understood the purpose of life and lived it: They loved.

Question #128

"Living another life as a dolphin or even another human sounds cool to me. Why doesn't the Church believe in reincarnation after death?"

A. Though living as a dolphin or as another human being might sound cool from a certain perspective, we need to remember that we are more than disembodied spirits floating in a particular body; we are not "ghosts in the machine." We are unique body-soul *persons* made in God's image and likeness. Each and every human person is "unrepeatable," to use an expression of St. John Paul II. So, our bodies are as much of who we are as our souls. Our human bodies express our personhood—showing forth the persons we have been created by God to be.

Reincarnation implies that the essence of humanity lies in our spiritual component and that our bodies are unimportant. But the incarnation of Jesus shows this to be false. He became a true man at a particular moment of human history; he was born of the Virgin Mary, receiving from her a human nature with all that goes with it: the color of his eyes and hair, his height, and his personality.

It is not by accident that you were born into your family or that you have particular talents and gifts. You have always been in God's plan. As the Lord told the prophet Jeremiah,

"Before I formed you in the womb I knew you; and before you were born I consecrated you" (Jer 1:5). This is certainly an amazing thing: God has willed your existence—and every other human being that has ever lived or will live—from all eternity. You are destined to live eternally in heaven as the unique individual that you are.

Dolphins are cool, but God thinks you're cooler! Humans are not interchangeable with animals (or other humans, for that matter), and animals do not share equality with us in the eyes of God. This is why God created the earth and all the animals, and then gave Adam and Eve—representing all of humanity—dominion over all of it (Gn 1:26-28).

Question #129

"Where is heaven?"

A. Strictly speaking, since heaven is outside of space and time, it is "nowhere." Though we popularly speak of heaven as being "up" (somewhere above the clouds, in outer space or beyond the universe) and as hell being "down" (below the surface of the earth where there is a lot of fire and volcanic activity), these are just metaphors. No reasonable person actually believes that if we had the right kind of spacecraft and traveled far enough into outer space that we would find heaven. Nor would they believe that if we just dug in the right spot on earth and went down deep enough, that we would find hell. But just because heaven is outside the material realm of existence, this does not mean that it is less "real" than the reality we know on earth. In fact, heaven is the "most real" place there is. It is our true home, our destiny, the paradise to which God has called us to from all eternity. Heaven is the very reason why Jesus, the Messiah, was born, preached, suffered, died, and rose from the dead.

Question #130

"I think that because God is so loving and forgiving, everyone goes to heaven. What do you think about that?"

A. What you or I think about everyone going to heaven is irrelevant. The real question is: What does *God* think about it, and what has he revealed to us on the subject? If we take even a quick look at the New Testament, we find dozens of references to eternal life and how we attain it—through faith in Jesus and obedience to God's will (see CCC 161, 162). In all these passages, Jesus makes it clear that some will be saved while others will not. Here are just a few examples:

- In Matthew 7:13-14, Jesus tells his disciples to "enter by the narrow gate; for the gate is wide and the way is easy that leads to destruction, and those who enter it are many. For the gate is narrow and the way is hard that leads to life, and those who find it are few." In these verses, "destruction" affirms the reality of hell, the destination on the other side of the "wide" and "easy" gate. The road to "life," on the other hand, is the Christian Faith; it is "narrow" and "hard" because it requires discipline and self-sacrifice, the following of God's will rather than our own.

- Later in the same chapter of Matthew's Gospel, Jesus tells us what we need to do to be saved: "Not everyone who says to me, 'Lord, Lord,' shall enter the kingdom of heaven, but he who *does the will of my Father* who is in heaven" (Mt 7:21-23; emphasis added). So only those who do the will of God actually go to heaven; those who choose to disobey and reject his will do *not* go to heaven.

- Jesus says, "He who endures to the end will be saved" (Mt 10:22), implying that there are people who do *not* endure (i.e., persevere) in faith to the end of their lives. Some, tragically, will fall away from Jesus through sin and disobedience (see CCC 2088–2089).

- Speaking of the Last Judgment, Christ says to those who do not follow his will of serving others in this life, "Depart from me, you accursed, into the eternal fire prepared for the devil and his angels" (Mt 25:41). Hell is real, as Jesus' words indicate.

Though God is, as you say, "loving and forgiving," we must *ask* for his love and forgiveness. We must *choose* to accept the gift of salvation he is offering us—the gift of faith—and persevere by remaining in God's grace. But we are free to make our own choice. If we choose to do our "own thing" rather than "God's thing," he says, "OK, go right ahead, but know that there will be consequences." If we choose mortal sin over his grace, we are choosing to say "no" to his loving will. And in a profound confirmation of the awesome gift of freedom, he says, "*Your* will be done" (see CCC 1861). But only his will leads to salvation. So our destiny is in our own hands. Our constant struggle is to surrender our will to his will. In doing this, we show God that we love him above all things and truly want to be with him in heaven for eternity.

Question #131

"Since Satan got kicked out of heaven, does this mean that some people could still be damned after they go to heaven?"

A. No, thank goodness! This is an impossibility. If we die in a state of grace, we will be saved and go to heaven, either immediately or after some period of purification in purgatory. Once we enter heaven, our hearts will be confirmed in God's love and we will be guaranteed to spend eternity in his presence.

Angelic decision-making is vastly different than ours, because the human intellect has been darkened and our human wills have been weakened by original sin. Satan, like all other angels, possessed a perfect intellect and will. Unlike human beings, who live in time and space, angels can see the full consequences of their decisions. So Satan knew that the result of his rebellion against God would be eternal exile from heaven. And still, he chose to rebel. That is why there is no possibility of repentance for him or any of the other fallen angels.

Question #132

"How long do people stay in purgatory before they go to heaven?"

A. This is a difficult question because the nature of "time" is different in purgatory than it is on earth. Purgatory—like heaven and hell—exists outside of space and time as we know it. In other words, their "time" is not like our "time," and it cannot be measured in the same way; it is "God's time." It might be more helpful to speak of the intensity (rather than the length) of suffering the souls in purgatory endure. Some people need greater purification than others, so the intensity of their suffering is greater. But remember—everyone in purgatory died in a state of grace and is destined for heaven (see CCC 1030). These souls willingly, even joyfully, endure their purification as a means of bringing their hearts closer to God, never experiencing *complete* torture like the souls in hell, because those in purgatory, however pained, are still bound for heaven. We can lessen the intensity of their sufferings through our own prayers and sacrifices, particularly by having Masses said for their intentions (see CCC 1032).

Question #133

"I heard a preacher on the radio say that there is no biblical basis for purgatory. Is the Catholic Church wrong to believe in it?"

A. Actually, the preacher you heard is wrong in saying there is no biblical basis for purgatory. But we can forgive his ignorance on the matter because the Bible he is using probably doesn't contain a key book that explicitly supports belief in purgatory, the second book of Maccabees.

This book, along with six other Old Testament books (Judith, Tobit, Sirach, Wisdom, Baruch, and First Maccabees), were removed from the Bible in the year 1519 by Martin Luther during the Protestant Reformation. The reasons for this removal are not important here, but it is important to point out that all Christians accepted all these books as inspired for the preceding 1,500 years.

In the second book of Maccabees, we read that it is a "holy and pious thought to pray for the dead, that they might be loosed from their sin" (2 Mc 12:46). Though the word *purgatory* is not used here, the teaching about it certainly is.

A good way of explaining purgatory to non-Catholic Christians is to say something like this: "Jesus asks us to be perfect, as his heavenly Father is perfect. But I know that he still has quite a bit of work to do in me. The Bible tells us that we sin daily, and since nothing unclean will enter heaven (as it says in Revelation 21:27), we know that there can be no sin there. So Jesus must make us perfect. If we have not allowed him to make us perfect on earth, then he will finish the work of our sanctification before we enter heaven. This is why St. Paul says that some are saved, but only after passing through fire (1 Cor 3:15). This 'fire' is purgatory."

Purgatory is an application of the graces merited for us by Jesus on the Cross, so that we might be made pure before entering heaven. It can be thought of as the final stage of sanctification (i.e., the process of becoming holy). It is the application of the Blood of Christ to our souls, making us really pure. God does not simply *say* that we are pure—he makes us so, since his word accomplishes that which he intends (see Is 55:11). Purgatory does not add to or take away from the work of Jesus. It *is* the work of Jesus. It is one's immersion into the love of Christ, which removes the residue of imperfection from us (CCC 1030–1032).

The Bible tells us that God is like a "refiner's fire" (Mal 3:2). A refiner's fire burns all the corrosion and rust off of metals to make them shine with the fullest glory. Purgatory is God's "refining" or purification of souls that have died in his grace but still have "impurities" within them. It is not a second expiation (or atonement) for sin or a second chance for bad Christians. Rather, it is an application of the one perfect expiation of Jesus on the Cross; it is for those who die in God's grace but have not yet been made perfect.

Remember: Purgatory is *not* a third final destination for those who are not quite good enough for heaven or quite bad enough for hell. Everyone in purgatory will eventually enter the glory of heaven when their souls are ready. We can help them get to heaven more quickly by our prayers and sacrifices on their behalf.

Question #134

"What are indulgences?"

A. An indulgence is defined in the *Catechism* as "the remission before God of the temporal punishment due to sins whose guilt has already been forgiven" (CCC 1471).

To put it simply, an indulgence takes away any punishment we might still deserve as the result of a forgiven sin.

Every sin alienates us from God and our fellow Christians, and one act of repentance, though enough to gain us forgiveness, is often not enough to counteract the bad effects the sin has caused in ourselves or in the lives of others. For example, God forgave the sin of Adam and Eve, but he still punished them by kicking them out of the Garden of Eden (see Gn 3:17-19). This was a just punishment based on the gravity of their sin.

Here's an example from everyday life that might help: Let's say another teen steals your cell phone or laptop, and he gets caught. He is guilty of the crime of theft, and he could be sentenced to jail. But let's say it was his first offense, and because he is your age, you would feel bad if he went to jail. So you speak to—you *intercede* with—the judge not to sentence him to jail, but only to impose a fine, have him do a few hours community service, and make him return the stolen item. Your action helped lessen his punishment for the crime. An indulgence works in a similar way by lessening or even removing the punishment we need to suffer for a particular sin (see CCC 1471).

We need to remember that the Church is not merely a group of isolated individuals, all trying to get to heaven on their own. No, the Church is a *community* of believers, and each of us is called to help our fellow believers along the path of life. Our prayers, sacrifices, and good works can be offered up for the good of another, even to help them repair the damage caused by their sins. There is even more power in the communion of saints, in the prayers of Mary and the blessed souls in heaven, when they pray for us and intercede before God, the almighty Judge (see CCC 1477).

Indulgences are attached to the praying of certain prayers, devotions, or novenas, and are either *plenary* (full) or *partial,* depending on whether all the requirements the Church asks us to do are met (e.g., saying the prayer, receiving the Eucharist, and going to confession within a certain number of days). If all the requirements are met, then the indulgence is plenary; if not, then only a partial indulgence is earned. Also, to receive the indulgence, one must consciously ask to receive it.

Question #135

"What happens when a person goes to hell?"

A. Your question seems to be asking, "What is hell like?" Though the Church has defined certain aspects of the reality of hell, God has actually not revealed many of the details. Before we discuss these aspects, we need to say a few words about the existence of hell.

Many Christians today—including many Catholics—no longer believe in hell. Some hold that a place of eternal torment is incompatible with the love and mercy of a good God. But we cannot be united with God unless we love him, and we do not love him if we sin against him and others mortally (see CCC 1033). As St. John teaches, "He who does not love remains in death. Anyone who hates his brother is a murderer, and you know that no murderer has eternal life in him" (1 Jn 3:14-15). If we die in a state of mortal sin without repenting and accepting the merciful forgiveness God offers, we will be separated from him forever. This is not by his choice, but by ours. As unimaginable as it may seem, those who end up in hell have *chosen* to go there by their free choice (see CCC 1033).

The existence of hell is a dogmatic teaching of the Faith (see CCC 1033–1037). We are not free to dismiss it simply because it makes us feel uncomfortable. If someone does not believe in hell, this is no guarantee that he or she will not go there. In fact, willful disbelief in a dogma of the Church is objectively a mortal sin, and places one in danger of hell. But we should not be too fearful of this reality. Hell actually shows God's great love for us because it affirms our ability to freely choose or reject him.

Though the Bible and the teachings of the Church speak of hell as being "eternal fire," the greatest torment for the souls in hell is eternal separation from God (see CCC 1035). When a person goes to hell, he or she is forever cut off from God and feels an unbearable pain of loss. Other images used for hell in the Bible are "unquenchable fire" (Mt 3:12; Lk 3:17), "lake of fire" (Rv 20:15), "wailing (crying) and gnashing of teeth" (Mt 13:42, 22:13; Lk 13:28), and "darkness" (Mt 8:12, 22:13, 25:30).

Is hell an actual "place" or just a state of being? Our faith teaches us that at the end of time, at the General Judgment, our bodies will be reunited with our souls (see CCC 1038;

Jn 5:28-29). Though our bodies will be changed, they will still be made up of matter and must occupy space. So it would seem that hell will need to be a "place."

As wonderful as the peace of heaven will be, so also will the depth of despair be that is felt by a soul that goes to hell. We have been created for eternal union with God, and he alone can bring us happiness. So imagine the horror of a soul that realizes it is cut off from this happiness forever. There is only hate in hell, especially hatred of God. Because God is the source of light, life, and love, the absence of God will cause those in hell to shrivel up into the only thing that is left—themselves.

Question #136

"What sin is bad enough to warrant someone going to hell?"

A. Any mortal sin is "bad enough" to kill the life of grace in our souls. Unfortunately, there are many objectively mortal sins: murder, adultery, fornication, stealing, deliberate drunkenness, disrespect to parents (see Mark 10:19), and the list goes on. Of course, for a person to be truly guilty of sinning mortally, the three requirements we have discussed previously must be met: (1) grave matter (such as the sins we just mentioned); (2) full knowledge that the sin is objectively mortal; and (3) full consent of the will. One cannot sin mortally by accident, so one cannot go to hell by accident. It must be a free choice.

Naturally, all sins can be forgiven if we sincerely turn to God and repent before the moment of death. In this sense, there is no sin that is beyond God's forgiveness. You may have heard of the "sin against the Holy Spirit" as being the only unforgivable sin, but this is not an action. Rather, sinning against the Holy Spirit is actually persisting in one's sins until death—it is the sin of final impenitence. It is a final saying "no" to God. And God says, "I have given you freedom, and I accept your decision. You obviously do not want to be in my presence, so I will send you where you want to go."

Also, there are two important things about the Catholic teaching on hell we need to keep in mind:

1. God predestines no one to go to hell; an act of willful disobedience—a mortal sin—is needed, along with a failure to seek his forgiveness and grace in the sacrament of reconciliation. In other words, to go to hell, we must sin mortally and persist in that sin until death (see CCC 1037).

2. We are forbidden to say—or even speculate—that a particular person is in hell. We are not in a position to judge the state of anyone's soul at the moment of death. Only God has that job. All we *are* required to affirm is the *possibility* of someone being condemned to hell.

Question #137

"Could Satan or the other fallen angels ever repent?"

A. No, and this is not because God is lacking in mercy. The reason they cannot repent is rooted in their very nature as angels. Satan (or "the devil") and the other fallen angels (often called "demons") were created naturally good, but they became evil through a choice against God that was final and irreversible (see CCC 391, 393). Their act of rebellion is *irrevocable* (that is, it cannot be taken back) because they possess a perfect angelic intellect, which, unlike human intellect, is not darkened by ignorance. They could clearly see the true nature of their choice and all the consequences that would flow from it. As a result, their rebellion against God and his will was definitive. So, as the *Catechism* teaches, "There is no repentance for the angels after their fall, just as there is no repentance for men after death" (CCC 393).

Remember: Satan is only a creature; he is not God's "opposite." Being omnipotent, God has no opposite. Though Satan (and the other demons), like all angels, is powerful and has an intellect that far surpasses our own, we need not be afraid of him if we are in God's grace. Why God permits the activity of Satan is a "great mystery," but we know that cannot prevent God from fulfilling his will for man (see CCC 395). In the end, St. Paul tells us that "in everything God works for good with those who love him" (Rom 8:28). Through temptation, our wills can be strengthened to follow Jesus more faithfully and grow in holiness. Whenever we encounter a strong temptation by Satan, we can pray to Our Lady for strength, or pray the powerful prayer of St. Michael:

> *St. Michael the Archangel, defend us in battle. Be our protection against the wickedness and snares of the Devil. May God rebuke him, we humbly pray, and do thou, O prince of the heavenly host, by the power of God, cast into hell Satan and all the evil spirits who prowl throughout the world seeking the ruin of souls. Amen.*

Question #138
"Can people really get possessed by evil spirits?"

A. Yes. Though some people today may think such a belief is ridiculous, a relic of the Middle Ages, the possibility of demonic possession has always been taught by the Church. Even a quick reading of the New Testament shows that Jesus expelled "unclean spirits" from people on many occasions (see Mt 4:24, 8:16, 9:32, 12:22, 15:22; Mk 1:23-27, 5:2-4, 9:17, 16:9; Lk 8:2, 8:30ff).

Regarding demonic possession, we need to be careful and not mistake the Hollywood portrayals in movies such as *The Exorcist* for the real thing. True demonic possession is rare. The Church is extremely cautious in determining that someone is truly possessed. It requires the testimony of various experts—in particular, doctors and psychiatrists—to rule out physical or psychological illness. In addition, the person thought to be possessed must demonstrate extraordinary abilities, such as unusual physical strength, knowledge of a language he or she never studied, levitation, etc.

Every diocese has a priest designated by the bishop to be its official exorcist. The name of the exorcist is usually kept secret for his own protection. He must be a man of great holiness, have been ordained for many years, and be well-schooled in theology.

Question #139

"What is the Catholic Church's position on believing in ghosts?"

A. Given our society's current interest in "supernatural" phenomena, this is an important question. Some people reject the idea of ghosts as crazy or superstitious, putting them on the same level as werewolves, vampires, or extraterrestrials. But let's take a look at what Catholic teaching has to say on the matter.

Before we can ask whether ghosts exist, we need to be clear on what we're talking about. A "ghost," according to the definition found in Webster's New Collegiate dictionary, is a "the soul of a dead person, a disembodied human spirit." So a ghost is *not* an angel or a demon; rather, it is that part of a human being—the soul or spirit—which is separated from the body at death. So everyone now in heaven, hell, or purgatory could be called a "ghost," and this will be the case until the Last Judgment, when our souls will be reunited with our bodies (see CCC 1038). In this sense, we as Catholics affirm that "ghosts" exist.

The real question is whether or not ghosts can appear on earth. Both Scripture and the testimony of the saints seem to indicate that they can. In First Samuel 28:3-20, we read how the spirit of the deceased prophet Samuel appeared to King Saul, and in Second Maccabees 15:11-16, Judas Maccabeus was visited by the dead prophet Jeremiah, who handed him a golden sword. During the Transfiguration, Moses and Elijah appeared to Jesus and the apostles Peter, John, and James on the mountain (Mt 17:1-3). In Catholic tradition, Pope St. Gregory the Great in the sixth century AD wrote about numerous appearances of canonized saints or recently deceased holy men and women, and there is a well-documented appearance in 1836 of a seminary student who had died the day before to St. John Bosco and twenty seminarians. More recently, St. Pio of Pietrelcina (also known as Padre Pio, 1887–1968) is said to have appeared to people on several occasions.

So, while we can affirm that ghosts can appear on earth, it is certainly true that most stories of "hauntings" (or houses that are said to be "haunted") by ghosts have *natural* explanations. As extraordinary supernatural phenomena, true appearances of ghosts are not everyday occurrences. Remember—God is in charge of the universe, and if the spirit of a deceased human being appears on earth, it is because he permits it.

Question #140

"Catholics acknowledge that Jesus is the 'one mediator' between God and man. But we also believe we can pray to saints. Isn't this a contradiction?"

A. No, it is not a contradiction at all. When we ask the Blessed Virgin Mary or one of the saints to pray for us, we are simply asking for their intercession before God as someone who is in his presence. While we can always pray to Jesus directly, we can also walk with the Lord accompanied by the intercessory prayers of his saints in heaven. We should rejoice that God has given us the powerful gift of their prayers.

Just as the prayers of other Christians on earth are powerful, we ask those who have gone before us in faith to intercede for us as well. As St. Paul says in his first letter to Timothy, "First of all, then, I urge that supplications, prayers, intercessions, and thanksgivings be made for all men … that we may lead a quiet and peaceable life, godly and respectful in every way. This is good, and it is acceptable in the sight of God our Savior, who desires all men to be saved and come the knowledge of the truth" (1 Tm 2:1-4).

Here are some other passages of Scripture which support the time-honored practice of asking the saints, our "fellow citizens" (Eph 2:19) to pray for us:

- Those in heaven are part of the mystical body of Christ. They have not been separated from us by death but surround us as a "great cloud of witnesses" (Heb 12:1).

- Those in heaven stand before the throne of God and offer our prayers to him (Rv 5:8), and cheer us on as we run the good race. If they are offering our prayers to God, as the Bible says, that must mean that God has enabled them to know what our prayers are.

- In the letter of St. James we read how the "fervent prayer of a righteous man" is very powerful (Jas 5:16). Those in heaven are surely righteous, since nothing unclean can enter heaven (Rv 21:27).

Praying for the intercession of the saints does not diminish Christ's role as the one mediator—it shows it more clearly. Those in heaven have a perfected love, so how could they not intercede for us? Christ is the vine and we are the branches, so if we are connected to him, we are inseparably bound together as well.

Heaven is not an isolated part of the body of Christ. The saints in heaven have traditionally been called the *Church Triumphant.* Has the union of the saints with God caused them to forget about the rest of the body of Christ? This wouldn't make sense, since the closer we get to Christ here on earth, the more we become aware of and are concerned about the needs of others. When we are perfected in love in heaven, it is safe to assume that we will not forget about our earthly family.

Question #141

"Someone told me that it is useless to pray to saints because no one is conscious after death. Where in the Bible does it say that people are conscious after they die?"

A. Perhaps the best passage can be found in the first letter of Peter, which talks about Jesus' descent into Hades, the place of the dead. The apostle tells us how Jesus "preached to the spirits in prison" (1 Pt 3:19). If the dead were unconscious, then to whom would Jesus have been preaching? Similarly, St. Peter explains that the "good news was declared also to the dead" (1 Pt 4:6).

If the dead are "asleep," we need to ask how Jesus communicated with them during his transfiguration (Mt 17:1-5), how they offer our prayers to God (Rv 5:8), how they cry out in a loud voice in praise of God (Rv 7:10), how they "serve him day and night" (Rv 7:15), and how the souls of the martyrs in heaven cry out, "How long will it be, holy and true master, before you sit in judgment and avenge our blood on the inhabitants of the earth?" (Rv 6:10). Those who have died are *more* alive than we are, not less, and they surround us as a great cloud of witnesses (Heb 12:1). Also, St. Paul tells us he would rather depart this life to be with Christ (Phil. 1:23), not that he longs to depart this life so he can take an endless nap.

Question #142

"My aunt says that the Bible condemns contacting the dead. So isn't it wrong for Catholics to pray to saints?"

A. In one sense, your aunt is right. The Bible does forbid summoning dead spirits or trying to communicate with them through mediums (see Lv 19:31; Dt 18:9-15). This is known as *divination,* a word that you can see has "divine" as its root. In doing these things, a person tries to be like God. As the *Catechism* teaches, "All forms of divination are to be rejected ... conjuring up the dead or other practices supposed to 'unveil' the future. Consulting horoscopes, astrology, palm reading, interpretation of omens and lots, the phenomenon of clairvoyance, and recourse to mediums all conceal a desire for power over time, history … and other human beings. *They contradict the honor, respect, and loving fear we owe God alone"* (CCC 2116; emphasis added). This being said, there is an enormous difference between asking for the intercession of the saints and having a séance!

The difference lies in the *intention* of the activity. When a person consults a medium or a psychic to contact the dead, he or she is trying to gain power over the forces of nature—or, more precisely, *super*-nature—for their own purposes rather than for God's purposes.

When we pray to the saints, we are asking for their prayers before God that his will be done, not ours. Our prayers to the saints bear great fruit because they stand in God's presence and can intercede for us. This is vastly different than trying to contact or conjure up the spirits of deceased loved ones.

During the Transfiguration, Jesus himself spoke with Moses and Elijah. We need to recall that those in heaven are *more alive* than those of us on earth. As Jesus says, God is Lord of the living, not of the dead (Mk 12:26-27; Lk 20:37-38).

Question #143

"How can Mary, not being omniscient or omnipotent like God, simultaneously hear the prayers of everyone throughout the world?"

A. The simple answer to your question is this: Mary does not need to be omniscient (that is, all-knowing) or omnipotent (all-powerful) to hear our prayers. Here's an analogy from everyday life. You could be connected with several—or even dozens or hundreds—of people via a videoconference or conference call, but this does not require you to be omnipotent. If technology is able to allow large numbers of people to communicate from literally anywhere on earth, God could easily grant Mary the ability to hear and answer our prayers, many though they be.

Of course, hearing the prayers of the faithful throughout the world would require a greater capacity of perception than we experience on earth. Since Mary, now in heaven, is *outside* of time, she has eternity to offer each petition to her Son. So the sheer number of prayers directed to her is not a problem, heavenly speaking.

This ability to hear the prayers of those on earth also applies to the other saints as well. How so? The Bible tells us that when we get to heaven, we shall know fully, even as we are fully known (1 Cor 13:12). So our knowledge will be increased to the extent that God wishes to make it so. In the book of Revelation, we see that the people in heaven are very much aware of what is happening on earth. For example, Revelation 5:8 presents the image of the rising incense as "the prayers of the saints." From the context, it seems clear that these are intercessory prayers, prayers offered on behalf of believers on earth.

Those who have been saved and live in heaven have been perfected in love and are fully alive in Christ. To say that they are cut off from us reveals a misunderstanding of the body of Christ. The Church is not *three* bodies of isolated members—some on earth, others in heaven, still others in purgatory. All Christians make up *one* body, and the saints in heaven—especially Mary—truly desire us to be saved and join them. They *want* to intercede for us before the

Father so that we might be holy. If we choose to ignore them, it is our own loss.

Question #144

"What does it mean when Mary is called 'co-redemptrix'"?

A. The best way to understand this word is to break it into its parts. *Co* is from the Latin *cum,* meaning "with." In Latin, *trix* is a feminine suffix. So the word "co-redemptrix" literally means "the woman who redeems *with* the redeemer," or more precisely, the woman *assisting* the one who brings about redemption. It does *not* mean that Mary is somehow equal to Jesus, nor does it take away from his unique role as Savior of mankind.

Jesus is the one and only Redeemer. But just as Eve participated in Adam's Fall by her consent and pride, Mary, the "new Eve," joins in the work of our redemption by her humble consent to be the Mother of God. Mary's "yes" gave Jesus his body, and he offered this same body to his heavenly Father on the Cross, for her salvation and the salvation of all humanity. In the very act of redemption, Mary stood with the Redeemer at the foot of the Cross and joined her sufferings to his. As such, she stood "with the Redeemer," and can rightfully be called "co-redemptrix."

When accepted in a Christian spirit, all our sufferings can be redemptive. As St. Paul says, "I rejoice for your sake, for in my body, I make up what is lacking in the sufferings of Christ for the sake of the Church" (Col 1:24). At first, this sounds blasphemous. Weren't the sufferings of Christ sufficient to accomplish our salvation? Of course they were, but all of us need to be made holy, to be sanctified by Christ's grace. In theological terms, then, we can say that Jesus' death on the Cross is *sufficient* for our salvation, but that each of us must make this *efficient* in our lives by taking up our cross and following him every day. Joining our works and sufferings to the Cross of Christ unlocks its power in our lives and in the life of the mystical body of Christ—the Church.

So we can see that calling Mary "co-redemptrix" does not make her an equal to Jesus or in some way diminish his role as the sole Savior and Redeemer of mankind. It simply indicates the special role Mary played in salvation history. Nonetheless, care should be used when we use this term among non-Catholics, and we must be prepared to explain its meaning with clarity and charity.

Question #145

"What is the best way to explain Mary's immaculate conception?"

A. First, we need to realize that many people mistakenly think that the Immaculate Conception refers to Jesus' miraculous, virginal conception in the womb of Mary. It actually refers to the moment that Mary was naturally conceived in the womb of St. Anne, but was preserved from the stain of original sin by a unique grace of God (see CCC 491).

Second, we see in the New Testament that Gabriel greets Mary with the words, "Hail, *full of grace*" (Lk 1:28; emphasis added). The Greek word translated as "full of grace" is *kecharitomene*. The tense of this word means that Mary's "fullness of grace" was an action that had been completed in the past, *before* the appearance of the angel. So, according to the original language of the Gospel, the grace being spoken of here is not a *present* occurrence because of the Incarnation but is a condition perfected in Mary's *past.*

Third, we need to examine what Christians have believed on this question through the ages. Within the first four centuries of the Church, Mary was addressed by the Church Fathers as "all-holy," "the new Eve," "all-pure," "most innocent," "a miracle of grace," "purer than the angels," and "free from all stain of sin." Mary was seen as identical to Eve prior to the Fall, completely innocent and pure. This still begs the question, "Why?" Why did God preserve Mary from the stain of all sin? The answer is: So that she might be a worthy vessel to bear the God-man, Jesus Christ.

Interestingly, it was not only the Church Fathers who wrote in defense of the Immaculate Conception—several of the Protestant reformers did as well. Martin Luther stated, "In the very moment in which she began to live, she was without all sin"[24] Even the more radical reformer Zwingli added, "I esteem immensely the Mother of God, the ever-chaste, immaculate Virgin Mary ... It was fitting that such a holy Son should have a holy Mother." Even though these same men rejected many other Catholic teachings on Mary and the saints, they affirmed this very profound truth.

Question #146

"A Christian friend of mine told me that if the Blessed Mother had no sin, then she would not have needed a savior. He also said that nowhere in the Bible does it say that Mary was without sin. How can I respond?"

A. It would be a dangerous error to believe that Mary's Immaculate Conception in some way implies that she had no need of a savior. The Church certainly teaches that Mary *did* need a savior. However, Jesus saved Mary in a unique manner by *preserving* her from all sin, beginning at the moment of her conception (see CCC 491).

The following is a popular analogy used to help understand the truth of Mary's salvation. Imagine that you are walking down the street. Suddenly, you see a man fall down an open man-hole, full of sewage. He grabs onto the sides, and you go over and help pull him out. As you look up, you see a woman walking towards the same opening, about to fall in. You yell a warning for her and she stops. Thus, you save her from falling in. Which of the two did you save? Both of them. One you saved by pulling him out of danger; the other you saved from danger entirely. Similarly, Jesus saves both us *and* his mother. While he needed to pull us out of the pit of original sin, Jesus actually kept his mother from entering the pit at all. This is the essence of the Immaculate Conception. Jesus opens heaven to her as he does to us, just in a different manner (see CCC 492).

So Mary was preserved from sin by a "singular" (i.e., unique) grace of Jesus (see CCC 491). As mentioned previously, at the Annunciation, the angel calls Mary *kecharitomene* (Lk 1:28). This Greek word is a perfect passive participle, which literally means, "having been filled with grace." The tense indicates that it is an action that took place in the past but whose effects continue to the present. It indicates that Mary has been given an abundance of grace prior to the announcement of the angel, which was fitting to make her an appropriate dwelling place for Jesus. After all, the Old Testament tells us, "wisdom will not ... dwell in a body enslaved to sin" (Wis 1:4).

If he insists that the Bible does not explicitly say, "Mary did not sin," you could ask him to find the word *Trinity* in the Bible; the theological concept is clearly there, but the word is not. Or you could also ask him where in the Bible it says which books are inspired and should be included in it. It does not, but we trust the Church's authority on the matter. Not everything we need to know is explicit in Scripture, and the Bible does not teach that everything that should be believed is written down explicitly.

Question #147

"Why do Catholics consider Mary to be a queen?"

A. In the Old Testament, we see that kings from the line of David always had a throne positioned to the right of their own. This throne was reserved for a special person who wore a magnificent crown and served as intercessor before the king for the people of the kingdom. The king would even bow to her out of respect. This person was actually his own mother—the queen mother.

In 1 Kings 2, we see how the queen mother interceded for the people (see verses 17-19). We also see the king honored her (see verse 19), and her powerful role as intercessor was implied by the king's response: "Make your request, my mother, for I will not refuse you" (see verse 20). These examples give a general outline of the queen's role. In Jeremiah 13:18, we see that a union exists between the king and queen—they both wear crowns and sit on the same throne, and what happens to the king also happens to the queen mother. This tradition continued with all the Davidic kings.

This tradition continues in the person of Jesus. He is the "King of Kings," who was given the throne of his forefather

David forever. And his mother, Mary, is the Queen of Heaven. Of course, Jesus is the "King of Kings," and there is no other, so when he honors one member of the Church, we are obliged to share the joy (1 Cor 12:26). It is a simple fact that Jesus gave honor and glory to Mary. This is because by becoming man, Jesus was under the commandment to honor his mother and father. The Hebrew word for honor is *covodah*. This is not merely a tipping of the hat but a bestowing of honor and glory to another. Thus, since Jesus is the only Son who has the power to honor his mother with a crown of twelve stars (see Rv 12), He does so. Most of us would do the same, and the Church imitates Jesus by honoring Mary as a queen.

Question #148

"How could Mary have been a lifelong virgin if Jesus had brothers?"

A. You probably are thinking of Matthew 13:55, which mentions "the brethren" (or "brothers") of Jesus and lists them by name. This passage has been a source of controversy since the time of the Protestant Reformation of the sixteenth century. Before that time, Mary's perpetual virginity was universally believed, both by the Catholic and Eastern Orthodox Churches. Interestingly, even some of the Protestant reformers, notably Martin Luther, affirmed Mary's perpetual virginity.

We always need to keep in mind that the Bible was not written in English. In the original Greek of the New Testament, the word *adelphoi,* which is commonly translated "brothers," was used to refer to blood brothers, step-brothers, uncles, cousins, nephews, neighbors, fellow workers, and kinsmen. We see this in the Middle East today and in our own culture, in which many ethnic groups use the term "brother" to refer to any male members of their race or ethnicity. In Acts 1:15, St. Luke refers to 120 "brothers," and it is clear they were not born of the same mother!

This was also the case in the original Hebrew of the Old Testament. For example, in the book of Genesis, Lot and Abraham, as well as Jacob and Laban, are called "brothers." This is meant in a general sense, because other passages indicate they were related as nephews and uncles (see Gn 14:14, 11:26-28, 29:15).

Another powerful affirmation of Mary's perpetual virginity occurs at the foot of the Cross. Looking down at his mother just before he died, Jesus handed her over into the care of St. John the Apostle: "'Woman, behold, your son!' Then he said to the disciple, 'Behold your mother.' And from that hour the disciple took her to his own home'" (Jn 19:26-27). According to Jewish custom, if Jesus had blood brothers, the care of his mother would have passed to them rather than to St. John.

Question #149

"In Matthew's Gospel, it says, "But he [Joseph] knew her [Mary] not until she had borne a son, and called his name, Jesus" (Mt 1:24-25). Doesn't this imply that Mary and Joseph had marital relations after Jesus was born?"

A. Not at all. The Greek word for "until" is *heos,* and it does not imply a change in condition or situation. For example, in 2 Samuel 6:23, we read, "Michal, the daughter of Saul, had no children *until* the day of her death." (She obviously didn't have any children after that either). Matthew used the word *heos* in the same sense. He was only concerned with what happened before the birth of Christ—to show that Jesus was born of a virgin. So, based on the original Greek, it is a false inference to use the New Testament to support the idea that Joseph and Mary engaged in sexual relations or had other children. The text simply does not support this.

In addition, one would be going up against 1,500 years of unwavering tradition, the unanimous opinion of the Fathers of the Church, and, most importantly, the solemn definition of Mary's perpetual virginity, which we express within the context of the penitential rite at Mass, "and I ask blessed Mary, *ever virgin*, all the angels and saints, and you, my brothers and sisters, to pray for me to the Lord our God" (Order of Mass, Penitential Rite, Option A; emphasis added).

Question #150

"Are we allowed to have statues of Mary and the saints? I heard that there is a verse in the book of Exodus that condemns this practice. Is that true?"

A. The Bible condemns the *worshiping* of statues; this would be idolatry. But even in the Old Testament, we can see the difference between the creation of a "graven image" (i.e., a pagan idol) and the legitimate figures ordered by and pleasing to God. For example, Moses made two golden angels (Ex 25:18) and a bronze serpent (Nm 21:4-9), while Solomon ordered that two wooden angels be put in the Temple (1 Kgs 6:23). And the Temple was filled with images of creatures from heaven and earth. This demonstrates that God is not opposed to the actual images being made as long as we do not idolize (i.e., worship) them.

By the way, the practice of honoring images of Jesus, Mary, and the saints was challenged throughout the early centuries of the Church by various heretical movements. This question was definitively settled by the second council of Nicea in AD 787 (see CCC 1160, 1161).

Question #151

"Where in the Bible does Jesus give us a pope?"

A. In the sixteenth chapter of Matthew, Jesus asks his apostles, "Who do men say that the Son of Man is?" (verse 13). After hearing a variety of answers, he puts the question directly to the apostles, "Who do *you* say that I am?" (verse 15). Simon Peter is the one who responds without hesitation, "You are the Christ, the son of living God" (verse 16). Jesus then grants him ultimate authority in the Church by saying, "Blessed are you, Simon Bar-Jona! For flesh and blood has not revealed this to you, but my Father who is in heaven. And I tell you, you are Peter, and on this rock I will build my church and the powers of death shall not prevail against it" (verses 17-18). In these words, Jesus established Peter as head of the apostles, entrusting him with a unique teaching authority (see CCC 552).

In Matthew 16:19, Jesus further specifies this unique authority given to Peter using the images of "keys" and "binding and loosing": "I will give you the keys of the kingdom of heaven, and whatever you bind on earth shall be bound in heaven, and whatever you loose on earth shall be loosed in heaven." Here, Jesus grants Peter the power to absolve people of their sins, to teach definitively in his name, and to make disciplinary laws for the Church (see CCC 553). This is when Jesus gave us our first pope and created the office of the papacy that would be passed down through the ages in an unbroken line of succession leading to the current pope.

Question #152

"I know Catholics say that Peter was 'the Rock,' but a friend told me that the Greek word used for Peter actually means 'small rock.' Therefore, how can Peter be as important as Catholics make him out to be?"

A. In one respect, your friend is right—we need to look to the original Greek of the New Testament to determine the literal meaning of these words. In Matthew 16:18, the Greek words *petros* and *petra* appear when Jesus is giving Simon his new name, Peter. Some say that *petra* means "big rock," and *petros* means a small one. But this is beside the point. The real difference between these words only exists because *petra* is a feminine noun; Jesus could hardly have applied a feminine form to Simon. So Jesus calls Simon *petros,* because this is the masculine equivalent of *petra.* Both mean "rock."

Another key point to remember regarding this question is that the New Testament was written in Greek, but Jesus actually spoke Aramaic. In this language, there is no change in gender at all. So the above passage would read: "You are *kepha* (rock) and on this *kepha* (rock) I will build my church." To argue against the primacy of Peter or the unique role he was given in the Church by Jesus based on the Greek of Matthew 16:18 is a very weak argument.

Finally, it is important to realize that Peter's name is mentioned 190 times in the New Testament, over 150 times more often than any other apostle! Also, Peter is always mentioned first in the biblical lists of apostles. These are not accidents; Peter was the unique leader of the Church, and the apostles and other first-century Christians knew it. Catholics make Peter out to be very important because, well, he is!

Chapter 9

CATHOLIC MORALITY

Question #153

"Why are some Catholics opposed to dating? If teens are not supposed to date, how can you get to know someone?"

A. In the United States and other parts of the Western world, dating is a very recent practice. Until the early twentieth century, *courtship* was the preferred manner in which a man and a woman got to know each other in preparation for marriage. In courtship, the couple rarely— if ever—was alone together; they were usually in the company of family members.

You are correct that some Catholics and non-Catholics alike have expressed concerns about the modern practice of dating. The dramatic increase in sexual activity among teens since the 1960s—along with an increase in the number of teen abortions and sexually transmitted diseases—goes hand-in-hand with the rise in the popularity of dating. The reasons for this are not hard to see: Dating offers an opportunity for young men and women to be alone together, something the older practice of courtship avoided. Many argue that allowing two young people to *date* each other—with extended amounts of time by themselves—is ultimately not in the best interest of those two people.

If you think about it, the idea that it is impossible to get to know someone unless you spend a lot of time alone with them is actually pretty crazy. Most of us have friends that we know very well and never dated! Getting to know someone happens in many ways, but especially when we hang out with others and do things together that naturally lead to friendship.

The time of exploration that occurs before actually "going out" with a person usually happens in groups, on the phone, at sporting events, group trips to the movies, and hanging out at coffee shops. Even though there is not an intense amount of alone time spent, you are getting to know the person. This is healthy and helps you learn a lot about the opposite sex without actually dating.

There are some significant advantages to courtship over dating. For example, courtship helps the couple preserve their chastity by meeting during social gatherings or in the presence of family members. On the other hand, in dating, a couple can easily become too close, too fast—both physically and emotionally—even though neither person is prepared to make the kind of lifelong commitment to the other that should accompany such intimacy. Before long, one person decides to get out of the relationship, often leaving the other feeling hurt and abandoned. Such feelings are natural because God made it this way. When a man and woman become close, an intense emotional bonding begins to occur. This emotional bonding helps to nurture, preserve, and sustain the relationship and only grows more intense when a couple becomes physically involved. Because this bonding is so powerful, it is intended to occur only within marriage, when two people *are* prepared to commit themselves to each other for life. Practicing courtship rather than dating can, in this way, prevent unnecessary hurts and lessen the emotional baggage that one brings into marriage.

In any discussion about dating, it is important to understand the primary purpose for a young man and a woman to get together in the first place. All of us are called by God to a particular state in life, a vocation. If we believe we are called to be married, part of finding out about this vocation must involve spending time in the company of someone we think would make a good husband or wife. The more "low-risk" types of relating ("talking," etc.) that you can practice before college, the better your habits will be when you get out on your own and try to live a life of purity on a college campus that may sometimes more resemble "hook-up city" than a place to grow intellectually and emotionally. Exploring the opposite sex in less intense, less formal ways that are fun (but leave you without emotional baggage) will prepare you well for later discernment of marriage through a more intense, exclusive relationship.

In the end, whether you decide to date or not, the important thing is to be aware that the more time you spend alone with someone, the more intense things will probably get. If spending time alone with someone is making it harder for you to be the person of purity God calls you to be, then being wise and setting time boundaries and favoring group dating over "going solo" can be a very good thing.

Question #154

"Is it OK to date someone who is not a Christian?"

A. Yes, but if you're really serious about your Catholic faith, dating a non-Christian is filled with potential difficulties.

Your belief in Christ should shape who you are as a person—your attitudes towards other people, the world, money, children, etc. While someone of a non-Christian faith tradition may be kind, generous, and morally good, he or she still does not fully share your view of the world.

Since the ultimate goal of dating is finding the right marriage partner, you should consider dating someone who is on the same spiritual path as you. The Bible supports this: "Do not be mismated [i.e., joined or married] with unbelievers. For what partnership have righteousness and iniquity?" (2 Cor 6:14) When looking for a spouse, most people look for someone who has similar interests and goals. Hopefully, your faith is your most serious interest, and making it to heaven is your most serious goal. In light of what Scripture is telling us, it seems wise to date someone who believes like you do and worships the God you worship.

Question #155

"My parents don't like the guy I'm dating. Is it right for them to tell me to stop dating him?"

A. Assuming you are under eighteen or are living at home with your parents, the answer is yes. According to the *Catechism of the Catholic Church,* "as long as a child lives at home with his parents, the child should obey his parents in all that they ask of him when it is for his good or that of the family. 'Children, obey your parents in everything, for this pleases the Lord'" (CCC 2217; Col 3:20; cf. Eph 6:1).

Being a good parent is not easy. Parents must often make difficult decisions that are unpopular with their children. Your parents love you very much and truly want what is best for you. A loving parent is always concerned about the people their children spend time with, especially those they are dating. A parent who does not monitor their child's choice of friends and choice of dates is not doing his or her job. Although you may not always agree with your parents' decisions, you certainly owe them your love, obedience, and respect.

As young people become adults and move away from home, they usually become wiser, more mature, and more capable of making decisions independently, without their parents. But the *Catechism* reminds us that we "should continue to respect [our] parents. [We] should anticipate their wishes, [and] willingly seek their advice" (CCC 2217).

Question #156

"My friend is planning to move in with her boyfriend before they get married. How can I get her to see that this is a mistake?"

A. First of all, tell your friend about all the studies on the topic, which show that couples who "live together" before marriage have a much greater chance of divorce than couples who don't. Since the divorce rate in the United States is approaching fifty percent, the odds of her having a lasting and successful marriage decrease dramatically if she lives with her boyfriend prior to marriage.

When a man and woman exchange their wedding vows, they are promising to give themselves totally to one another—as the Bible puts it, "they become one flesh" (Gn 2:24; Mt 19:5; Mk 10:7). Marriage is based on the consent of spouses, on their will to give themselves to each other for life, to live a covenant of faithful and fruitful love (see CCC 1662).

God himself is the creator of marriage; it is so important and so sacred that Jesus made it a sacrament. There are two primary purposes of marriage: the love and well-being of the husband and wife, and the procreation and upbringing of children (see CCC 2363). In order to realize these purposes, God has graced marriage with the beautiful gift of sexual love (CCC 2360). According to God's plan, it is only within marriage that this great gift can be properly shared, between a man and a woman who have given themselves to each other willingly, mutually, and completely (see CCC 2361).

Sexual relations between unmarried men and women are contrary to the very purpose of human sexuality and are an offense against the dignity of the persons themselves. Why? Because sex is meant to be a renewal of a couple's wedding vows. An unmarried couple, then, is actually speaking a "lie" with their bodies when they have sex.

When a couple decides to live together and engage in sexual relations, regardless of how firmly they intend to marry, they have not yet made a commitment to each other that would help ensure mutual sincerity and faithfulness in their relationship. This leaves the "live-in" couple open to the fickleness of their emotions and whims. So sexual activity is morally legitimate only when "a definitive community of life between a man and woman has been established" (CCC 2391). This is only realized through the total giving of self to another in marriage.

Therefore, genuine human love between a man and a woman cannot tolerate the "live-in" arrangement suggested by your friend. Rather, "it demands a total and definitive gift of persons to one another," that can only be fully realized through the solemn vows they exchange in marriage (see CCC 2391). During the months leading up to marriage, a couple "should see in this time ... a discovery of mutual respect, an apprenticeship in fidelity, and the hope of receiving one another from God. They should reserve for marriage the expressions of affection that belong to married love" (CCC 2350).

Question #157

"If nudity is natural then why is it wrong to look at pornography?"

A. Though nudity could be called "natural"—in the sense that we are born without clothing—it is definitely *not* natural for us to be walking around nude in public. Why is this? Is it because our bodies are bad or shameful? Not at all. Our bodies are holy creations of God; they are inherently good. In fact, it would be heretical to hold that the body is evil. However, our passions have become disordered because of original sin. This is why Adam and Eve covered themselves in fig leaves to hide their nakedness. It was not because their bodies were bad; it was because they were so good, they didn't want them exposed to the lustful look of the other. It is for the same reason that we wear clothing (aside from those cold winters). In a fallen age, seeing nakedness can easily lead us to lust.

Pornography is wrong because it degrades—rather than celebrates—the human body. This is the great difference between the nudity found in great works of art and that found in pornography. The true artist wants to celebrate the beauty of God's creation, but the pornographer only wants to arouse lust. Pornography leads to a warped view of sexuality. It causes us to view others as objects to be used, instead of as persons to be respected, cherished, and valued as unique individuals. Thus, it is wrong to look at pornography, not only because you are abusing your own gift of sexuality by indulging your sexual desire selfishly, but also because you are strengthening a habit of selfishness that will eventually harm your relationships with others. Also, pornography can become addictive and lead to perverse sexual behaviors, which further degrade those involved.

Question #158

"How can I overcome my addiction to Internet pornography?"

A. There are three important steps you can take to overcome this devastating addiction:

1. *Pray.* Purity of heart and mind is impossible without an active prayer life. Ask God for mercy and grace, particularly in times of temptation. Ask Our Lady and St. Joseph to intercede for you.

2. *Arm yourself* with the "spiritual weapons" Jesus has given us to grow in holiness. These include attending Mass daily (or as often as possible), going to confession on a regular basis (even weekly), praying the Rosary, meditating on the Stations of the Cross, making visits the Blessed Sacrament, or a weekly holy hour, and fasting. These practices will give you spiritual discipline, increase your willpower, and supply you with the much-needed grace to fight your addiction.

3. *Find a spiritual director* you can speak to regularly and to whom you can be accountable. Listen carefully to his direction, and strive to put his recommendations into practice.

You can also:

- Place holy objects or pictures around your computer. They will catch your attention and keep you focused on the things of God.

- Keep yourself busy, because you're more likely to be tempted when you're bored. Go to the gym, visit some friends, jog around the block, etc.

- Set reasonable goals for yourself. If you have been looking at pornographic web sites three times a week, make a commitment to go an entire week without looking at them at all. When the week is over, you will have a sense of confidence and a desire to persevere longer. Keep this up until the habit is overcome.

- Place an Internet filter on your computer, or sign up with an Internet service provider that filters inappropriate material as part of its normal service. And have someone else keep the password.

- For a time, you may even need to disconnect your devices from the Internet. To paraphrase Jesus' words in the Gospel: If your computer or phone causes you to sin, disconnect it; it would be better to enter into heaven with a broken phone than to be thrown into Gehenna.

- Realize that you are not alone. Many others are struggling with a similar addiction. The good news is that there are support groups available that can be of enormous help.

Trying to overcome your addiction without doing the above things is like waving the white flag of surrender, because you are helpless. You can overcome this sin with God's grace. Take it one day at a time.

Question #159

"Where in the Bible does it say that masturbation is wrong?"

A. In Genesis, there is a specific condemnation of "spilling one's seed" when Onan withdrew himself during intercourse and "wasted his seed on the ground" (Gn 38:9). The Scriptures go on to add: "What he did was displeasing in the sight of the LORD, and the Lord slew [he killed] him" (Gn 38:10). We can see by the severity of the punishment (death) that the Lord considered Onan's sin to be very serious. Other Scripture verses include 1 Corinthians 6:9 and Romans 1:24, both of which offer a general condemnation of irresponsible sex, of which masturbation is one type.

Masturbation is ultimately very harmful to a person's relationship with God and others. Though some modern psychologists hold that masturbation is harmless, that it is merely a part of adolescence, the Church has always taught that it is a disordered use of the great gift of our sexuality (see CCC 2352). Masturbation in the life of teenagers often becomes a form of sexual addiction, and while it is true that habit and immaturity may minimize the responsibility one has for this sin, it objectively remains a serious sin nonetheless.

Question #160

"I'm confused. Are teens allowed to kiss passionately?"

A. When you say "kiss passionately," we assume you mean more than just a short touching of the lips. Passionate kissing, while not necessarily sinful in itself, can arouse sexual feelings and lead to behaviors that are sinful. As a result, we would generally advise teens to refrain from this type of kissing. As we said in the answer to question 153, the main purpose of dating is to discover if you have a vocation to married life and, if so, whether the person you are dating would make a good husband or wife. Passionate kissing can cloud your judgment and light the flame of sexual desire—a desire that God intends to be fully expressed in marriage.

Question #161

"How can premarital sex be wrong if a couple is truly in love?"

A. The term "in love" is used very casually today. It often refers to an intense emotional attachment or infatuation with another person more than it does to "true love." So how can you tell if you "truly love" your boyfriend or girlfriend? You first need to understand something about the nature of love.

There are two important aspects to love. The first is the desire for union with another. The second is to do *what is best for the other.* Of these two aspects, the second is more important, and it should govern our desire for union with another. If physical union is more important than doing what is best for the other, then even rape could be considered loving. A couple who is having premarital sex desires union, but are they really willing to do what is best for the other? True love knows how to wait to *give;* lust can't wait to *get.*

God intends sex for marriage. Aside from the risks of sexually transmitted diseases (STDs), unplanned pregnancy, and the pain caused by gossip, premarital sex cuts one off from God. This is the *least* loving thing someone can do for the person they claim to "truly love." If a teenage boy *truly* loves his girlfriend, he should rather die than do anything that could harm her body or soul.

Many want the joys of marriage (i.e., sexual intimacy, the feeling of union with another) without the total commitment. When a couple has sex, they are saying, "I am entirely yours. I give myself completely to you." But an unmarried couple engaging in sex is speaking a lie with their bodies; they are saying that they are giving themselves to each other fully, but they really aren't. In order to truly love someone, we must be willing to speak the truth, whether that means being honest with our words or with our bodies. "True love" rejoices in the truth (see 1 Cor 13:6). That's why they call it "true" love!

Question #162

"Is it OK for a couple to use fertility drugs, hormones, and other methods if they have trouble having children?"

A. Infertility is a term that doctors apply to couples who have been trying to conceive a baby for one year or more without success. The term is also applied to couples who have tried without success for more than six months precisely during fertile times of the woman's cycle.

It is the role of medicine to treat physical dysfunction and promote proper bodily functioning. Sterility is a dysfunction of the reproductive system, while fertility is the proper function. So, the Church allows the use of fertility drugs. Also, such drugs must be used responsibly, since overuse of fertility drugs can cause a woman's ovaries to release too many eggs, causing multiple conceptions that are dangerous to both the mother and the babies.

A Catholic couple struggling with infertility should consult more than one source. The best thing for them to do is to consult with a good priest, a good Catholic doctor, and maybe even a good moral theologian. Unfortunately, not all Catholic doctors and priests can keep up with all the medical advances that scientists have been making in recent years. Reproductive technology is a specialized field, and just as you would not trust a decision about fertility to an ear, nose, and throat doctor, it would be unwise to ask moral advice of someone who is not well-educated on the topic.

It is a good thing that there are many options for couples to choose from, but just as it is their right to know what their fertility options are, it is also their duty to inquire earnestly about the truth of what all the options involve and what the Church teaches about each one. A good rule of thumb is to remember that the Church is in favor of *assisting* couples to become pregnant through the natural sexual act. There are many practices that seek to *replace the sexual act* with something else that achieves pregnancy, like *in vitro* fertilization. These practices are not morally acceptable for many reasons, one of which is that every child deserves to be the result of a loving embrace of his own father and mother.

Question #163

"How can contraception be wrong? Doesn't God want married couples to be responsible about how many children they have?"

A. In order to understand why contraception is wrong, we need to understand God's purpose for human sexuality. According to the *Catechism,* sexual love shared between a man and a woman within a properly recognized marriage is intended to fulfill two primary purposes: "the good of the spouses themselves and the transmission of life (having children). These two meanings or values cannot be separated without altering the couple's spiritual life and compromising the goods of marriage and the future of the family" (CCC 2363).

From the very beginning, we see these purposes revealed by God himself who tells us, "It is not good for the man [Adam] to be alone" (Gn 2:18). When God brings forth a "suitable partner" in Eve, Adam responds with joy by saying, "This [one] at last is bone of my bones and flesh of my flesh …" The Genesis author then tells us, "Therefore a man leaves his father and mother and cleaves [clings] to his wife, and they become one flesh" (Gn 2:23-25) Also in

Genesis, we see that "God blessed them, saying to them: 'Be fruitful and multiply, and fill the earth and subdue it'" (Gn 1:28). These passages give clear indication of God's design for human sexuality.

The problem with contraception is that it directly *contradicts* the openness to life that must be present in every sexual act. It actually goes against the inner truth of what sexual love *is*. When a couple uses contraception, they are telling God and each other that they are not interested in being open to life but are only interested in feeling close to each other and having physical pleasure together.

The *Catechism* further states that in having children and educating them, parents must "fulfill this duty with a sense of human and Christian responsibility. A particular aspect of this responsibility concerns the *regulation of procreation*. For just reasons, spouses may wish to space the births of their children" (CCC 2367–2368). In other words, there are valid reasons a married couple may responsibly and prayerfully decide to delay pregnancy at a particular time. For example, the family may be experiencing a particularly difficult financial situation after the loss of a job or one of the spouse's may be dealing with a serious health issue. By his own design, God has made it so that not every act of sexual intercourse results in the conception of a child. So there is a method known as natural family planning (NFP) by which a couple can attempt to regulate pregnancy if they have good reasons to do so. This method is perfectly moral and in line with the teaching of the Church because it honors God's divine plan.

NFP is a method that monitors a woman's natural cycle of fertility and infertility and then uses the information as a gauge which can help a couple to periodically avoid conception, in a manner that is morally acceptable. NFP also pinpoints the times of the month when a woman is most fertile, thus giving the couple a gauge by which they can have the most success in trying to achieve pregnancy as well. The *Catechism* assures us that such methods "respect the bodies of the spouses, encourage tenderness between them, and favor the education of an authentic freedom" (CCC 2370). But the *Catechism* goes to great lengths in explaining that it is the couple's "duty to make certain their desire is not motivated by selfishness but is in conformity with the generosity appropriate to responsible parenthood" (CCC 2368).

It must be emphasized that the decision to use NFP to avoid pregnancy must be made only after a lot of thought, reflection, and prayer. If a couple is having difficulty figuring out God's will in this area of their lives, seeking the counsel of a good spiritual director (i.e., a priest who upholds the teachings of the Church on this matter) is a wise idea.

Question #164

"If teens are going to have sex anyway, isn't it better for them to use contraception than to spread disease or get pregnant?"

A. In recent years, the misguided notion contained in your question has been made by many liberal educators and health advocates, and it has actually succeeded in shaping certain aspects of American public health policy. For example, a number of school districts throughout the country now make contraceptive devices (particularly condoms) available free-of-charge to their high school students. Not surprisingly, the implementation of such policies has *not* resulted in reducing the spread of sexually transmitted diseases (STDs) or the number of teen pregnancies. In fact, we continue to see the kinds of alarming statistics associated with STDs, out-of-wedlock pregnancy, and abortion that have plagued our society for many years.

By giving teens the license to participate in illicit behavior by distributing contraceptives, schools are just increasing the likelihood of such behavior among teens. This deplorable fact is only made worse when we consider the false sense of security that contraception helps foster. For instance, the most commonly transmitted STD is Human Papillomavirus (HPV), which is killing more American women than AIDS because it can lead to cervical cancer. However, according to the American Cancer Society, 'condoms cannot protect against infection with HPV.'"[25]

We hear a lot today about "safe sex." If we mean by this "using contraceptives," there is no such thing; it's just a myth. Not only does contraception not safeguard us from serious diseases, it does even less in preventing a heart from being broken or a soul from being lost. As we have already seen in previous answers, God has created the precious gift of human sexuality for a great, holy, and wonderful purpose—to bring new life into the world through the loving act of marital intimacy. This is the only true "safe sex." Or, even better—*"saved* sex"—sex used in the manner for which it has been created.

As human beings, we are gifted with free will, and so we have the capacity to freely choose to do what is right and to avoid that which is wrong. So the notion that "teens are going to have sex anyway," as if they have no choice in the matter, is totally false. Teenagers are not mere animals that only possess instincts; God gave humans (teens included!) the gift of *reason*—the ability to think and decide wisely. The fact is that teens, just like adults, can learn to live pure and chaste lives. God's grace is always there to help strengthen us to save the awesome gift of our sexuality for marriage. As St. Paul reminds us, we are capable of doing all things, "in him who strengthens [us]" (Phil 4:13).

Question #165

"If natural family planning and artificial birth control both prevent pregnancy, how are they different?"

A. Just by looking at the two names, we can see they are vastly different. *Contraception* is a word that means "against conception." Natural family planning is, well, about naturally planning the growth of one's family!

Here's an analogy which illustrates the huge difference between them:

A married man needs to support his family. He can do this one of two ways: by working at a legitimate job or by turning to a life of crime, robbing banks, for example. Either way, he's supporting his family, but does this make honest work the same thing as theft? Obviously not, even though both can be pursued for the same reason. As the old saying goes, the *end* does not justify the *means*.

Similarly, both natural family planning (NFP) and contraception can be used for the same reason—avoiding pregnancy. But this doesn't make them morally equal.

The end can be the same with both, but the means are very different.

NFP respects the good of procreation. It says that having a baby is, in itself, always a good thing, even if the circumstances at the moment may not be. It avoids bringing about the good of procreation for the moment but still allows the good of the unitive meaning of intercourse. NFP cooperates with the woman's natural cycle and doesn't alter the act of intercourse at all. The sexual act remains what it is—an act of love-giving; and the couples who engage in it are giving themselves fully to one another, withholding nothing of what they can give in the marital act. NFP is not *against* conception because it merely looks at the woman's fertility to help plan a family.

On the other hand, contraception doesn't respect the good of procreation. It treats new life as an evil to be avoided, rather than as a good which is inopportune to pursue at the moment (as with NFP). Contraceptive methods treat fertility as a hostile enemy to be defeated, not something with which one cooperates. And, as we have already said, contraception not only divides the "person-uniting" meaning of sex from the "person-begetting" meaning but also undermines the unitive aspect by deliberately withholding one's fertility in the act of intercourse.

There is one final point that can't go unmentioned. Many forms of contraception, such as the pill, the IUD, and "the shot," can act as *abortifacients* (i.e., cause abortions) by preventing a newly conceived human being from implanting in his or her mother's uterus. This reason alone should make anyone think twice before using contraception.

Question #166

"Should a teen couple get married if the girl gets pregnant?"

A. We must strive to do everything in our power—with the help of God's grace—to prevent such a situation from occurring in the first place. To this end, we need to stress the importance of the virtue of chastity. However, if two young people find themselves facing pregnancy, marriage may not be what is best for all parties, including the child.

When an unmarried girl becomes pregnant, there are a number of factors to be considered. For example, if the father of the child is someone the girl hardly knows or is someone who is unreliable or perhaps even abusive, marriage may worsen what is already a difficult situation. Too often, such marriages end in divorce.

Ideally, every child should have the benefit of a stable family life, complete with a mother and father who are married. This is why it is so important for us to follow God's blueprint for marriage and human sexuality from the start. Marriage is a serious matter, and a man and woman who enter into it should do so for the right reasons. If there are other motivating factors—no matter how well-intentioned—besides a genuine shared love and a sincere desire to make a lifelong commitment to one other, they would be better off not getting married. In such a scenario, placing the baby up for adoption is sometimes the best course of action.

Question #167

"I know that abortion is wrong, but what if the woman was raped? Would it be OK then?"

A. Rape is a horrible crime. As the *Catechism* notes, "it does injury to justice and charity ... [and] deeply wounds the respect, freedom, and physical and moral integrity to which every person has a right" (CCC 2356). A woman who has been a victim of rape has experienced one of the most traumatic experiences possible, and she often feels the pain of its emotional scars for the rest of her life.

The conception of a child in such a terrible circumstance can add to a rape victim's trauma. As a society, we must make certain that the victims of rape are given the compassion, healing, and support they so desperately need, especially those who have become pregnant as a result of being raped. The killing of the unborn child would add to the heinous nature of the crime. An abortion is another evil action that only creates another victim. In Catholic moral theology, there is actually a similarity between rape and direct abortion—they are both intrinsically evil acts that can never be justified.

Fr. Frank Pavone, director of Priests for Life, in an article on this topic, notes that "not only does abortion not alleviate the trauma of rape, but it brings about a trauma of its own. ... I know of women who have been raped and then had abortions, and are in counseling not for the rape but for the abortion! In rape, the trauma is 'Someone hurt me.' In abortion, the trauma is 'I hurt and killed someone else: my child.' That brings even more grief."

Fr. Pavone concludes by asking, "Why can't we extend to the child the same practical compassion, which we

[all] agree belongs to the woman? Why can't we expand the boundaries of those we welcome and care for? Why should helping and loving one (the mother) mean destroying the other (the child)? In reality, you cannot help one without helping the other, and you cannot hurt one without hurting the other."²⁶

Question #168
"Is it OK for a Catholic to be gay or lesbian?"

A. It depends on what you mean by "gay" or "lesbian." In common language in our country, the terms "gay" and "lesbian" are socio-political terms that are often used to refer to a specific lifestyle—one that includes being sexually active with members of the same sex. Obviously, we need to be careful what we're talking about here.

If you are asking if it is permissible, morally speaking, for someone to have homosexual attraction and desires, then the answer is "yes." Here we are talking about homosexual *orientation* (also called "same-sex attraction"), and the Church teaches that such an orientation is not sinful in itself—though it is disordered. The *Catechism* notes that while homosexuality's "psychological genesis remains largely unexplained" (CCC 2357), most homosexuals do not choose their attraction and find it a "trial" (CCC 2358). So we should always have compassion for those who are suffering with—and striving to overcome—their homosexual desires.

On the other hand, if you are asking whether it is OK to *act* upon one's same-sex attraction by experimenting in homosexual behaviors or engaging in an active homosexual lifestyle, then the answer is an emphatic "no." As the *Catechism* clearly states, homosexual acts are "intrinsically disordered" (CCC 2357). It is not OK, because the Church teaches that our sexuality is a gift, and God intends for that gift to be shared only within marriage. Those attracted to the same sex are called to chastity just as heterosexual people are.

Same-sex attraction is undoubtedly a difficult cross to bear. But with the grace offered by God through prayer and the sacraments, and with spiritual direction from a priest or another, living chastely can be achieved. Furthermore, the Church says that all its members should embrace those who carry this cross. We should love them, encourage them into active participation in the Church, and offer support to them as they struggle to remain sexually pure.

Many people who have previously lived a homosexual lifestyle have come to see the error of their ways and have embraced a life of chastity, and many are now happily married. Important work is being done to help in this area by groups such as Courage (Couragerc.org) and NARTH, the National Association for Research and Therapy of Homosexuality (Narth.com).

Question #169
"Why is it wrong for lesbians and gays to marry?"

A. Marriage and the family are the bedrock institutions of our society. The strength of a culture can be measured in accordance with the strength of its families. Due to a 2015 Supreme Court ruling, same-sex "marriage" is now legal in al U.S. states. In the eyes of the U.S. government, the common institution of the family as God created it—growing from the love of one man and one woman—is now one of many options. This will wreak havoc on

222 Did Jesus Have a Last Name?

society because God's way is the best way. Going against his plans hurts not only those homosexuals attempting to marry, but the entire culture in which they live.

As we have stated before, God has written into our sexuality a twofold purpose: it is (1) *unitive* and (2) *procreative*. By "unitive," the Church means that sex should be a "person-uniting" action. By "procreative," the Church teaches that God desires for sex between couples to be "person-creating" (or open to being so). Sexual acts that respect this twofold purpose are moral and good; those that do not are immoral and evil.

Homosexual acts, regardless of the intention of those who engage in them, cannot be truly unitive or procreative, so they cannot be moral and good in themselves. That they cannot be procreative is obvious; that they cannot be unitive becomes clear when we reflect on the matter a bit.

Homosexual acts cannot "unite" people in the true meaning of the word. No matter what homosexual persons may *claim* they mean by their actions, they cannot fully give themselves to each other in their acts as married people do. This is simply because the very acts they engage in are contrary to the natural law, which is God's eternal law manifested in his creation. For one thing, they cannot give a very important part of themselves to each other—their power to bring into existence with one's spouse a new life made in God's image.

Marriage is only possible between two persons of opposite sexes. Based on the physical design of man and woman, it is obvious that men and women were made to be together. Strictly speaking, then, "same-sex marriage" is an *impossibility;* the very words themselves have no meaning.

Marriage as a legal and social institution is intended to protect the family, especially to provide children with a stable, truly human environment in which to be conceived, nurtured, and educated. Homosexual couples are incapable of procreating naturally, and they don't provide a suitable environment for raising children because they lack the complementary nature of male and female love. Two moms do not equal a mom and a dad, nor do two dads.

Question #170

"What does the Church say about capital punishment?"

A. Imagine you are aboard a yacht for an ocean cruise when suddenly a storm comes up, sinking the yacht and stranding you on a desert island with a small group of survivors. You all get along at first, but one day, one of your former shipmates goes crazy and kills one of the other castaways. You catch the murderer and put him in a bamboo jail, but he eventually breaks out and kills someone else. In this scenario, as a way of protecting the others, you could legitimately condemn the man to death. In the same way, the Church recognizes that the state has the right to use deadly force in order to preserve the good of society. However, given that the prison systems in most developed countries are a sufficient way to punish criminals and keep them from harming society, the question arises as to whether capital punishment is *ever* necessary in modern society.

We are called by God to build a culture of life and a civilization of love. In the Old Testament, the Lord states, "Have I any pleasure in the death of the wicked, says the Lord God, and not rather that he should turn from his [evil] way and live? … Turn back from your evil ways!" (Ez 18:23, 33:10-11). In the New Testament, St. Peter writes, "The Lord is … forbearing [patient] toward you, not wishing that any should perish but that all should reach repentance" (2 Pt 3:9).

It is true that the Church has consistently upheld the right of the state to punish those who commit crimes. According to the *Catechism*, "Legitimate public authority has the right to inflict punishment proportionate to the gravity of the offense." In other words, for the sake of justice, the punishment imposed by the state should be on the same scale as the crime committed. The *Catechism* then explains that "the traditional teaching of the Church does not exclude recourse to the death penalty, if this is the only possible way of effectively defending human lives against the unjust aggressor" (CCC 2266-2267). So, the short answer is that the death penalty may be used as a last resort to protect society. [27]

Question #171

"If the death penalty would rid our society of murderers who may kill again, why is the Church opposed to it?"

A. As we have said, the intended purpose of the death penalty is to punish the guilty and protect society from dangerous criminals. The Church has always recognized the need for society to defend its citizens against the violence of aggressors, whether they are individuals or nations.

But what is the *best* way for society to protect itself from murderers? Advocates for capital punishment point out that there is a distinction between executing a person guilty of a serious crime and the murder of an innocent victim. They say that a killer who intentionally takes the life of an innocent person forfeits his "right to life." Death penalty supporters maintain that the only just punishment for murder is death, and that life imprisonment is too "soft." They also argue that capital punishment is a deterrent to potential murderers.

Recently, however, the Church has challenged us to look at this issue differently. St. John Paul II, while affirming the Church's traditional teaching on capital punishment, has asked governments to consider the key question: *What is the best way to build a "culture of life"?* The best way is not to return violence for violence, but to instill in society a greater appreciation for life in all its stages— from conception to natural death. Many would argue that executing murderers does little to help society promote a greater appreciation for life.

Even in extreme cases (such as an imprisoned murderer killing another prisoner or guard), the modern, bloodless means of imprisonment available in developed countries makes the possibility that a convicted killer would have the opportunity to kill again very remote. Such a criminal may be sentenced to solitary confinement or at least have his contact with others restricted. Bringing Christ's love to the world, along with good education and help for those in need, are better ways to rid societies of potential murderers. This would be true deterrence.

Question #172

"I feel very angry at the terrorist who attacked our country on September 11. Is this type of anger sinful?"

A. The *Catechism* teaches that anger is "an emotion which is not itself wrong, but which, when it is not controlled by reason or hardens into resentment and hate, becomes one of the seven deadly sins" (CCC glossary).

It is perfectly natural for us feel angry about the terrible tragedy of 9/11, which caused the death of thousands of our fellow citizens. This type of anger helps us to respond positively to the need to correct the wrong that was committed and to bring about justice. However, should that anger lead to hatred and the desire to harm others out of vengeance, then it becomes sinful. Anger that motivates us to condemn the actions of the people responsible for this horrific crime and bring them to justice is perfectly justifiable and could be called "righteous anger." Anger that causes hatred and stirs in us the desire for revenge is never justified.

Question #173

"My friend's church uses grape juice instead of wine at communion. He says that the Bible condemns the drinking of alcohol. Is this true?"

A. Although the Bible condemns *drunkenness*, it doesn't condemn drinking alcoholic beverages in moderation. After all, when considering the size of those six stone jars, Jesus probably multiplied 150 gallons of wine at the wedding feast of Cana (See Jn 2). Jesus came eating and drinking, and people accused him of being a glutton and a drunkard (Mt 11:19; Lk 7:34). This means that he drank wine that contained alcohol, as we see in John 19:29.

In Proverbs 31:6 and 1 Timothy 5:23, the Bible even recommends the drinking of wine. Also, at each Passover meal—the Last Supper Jesus had with his apostles was one such meal—three to four cups of wine would have traditionally been served. In none of the above instances is grape juice being served. It is clear from Jewish tradition and the practice of the early Church that the use of wine— and, by extension, other types of alcoholic beverages—is morally permissible.

Your friend may very well be a member of one of the Protestant denominations that took up an anti-alcohol position in the late nineteenth century and made it a key part of their beliefs. It was during this time that the *temperance movement* began in the United States, which eventually led to Prohibition (1920–1933), during which the sale and possession of alcohol was illegal throughout the country.

Question #174

"Is it OK to go to parties where underage drinking and wild behavior are going on as long as I'm not doing these things?"

A. The real question you should be asking yourself is: *Why would I want to go to such parties in the first place?* If "wild behavior" and "underage drinking" is happening and you are not joining in, how much fun would you really have anyway? Simply going to socialize is not a good answer. There are many other fun things you can do with your friends.

The situation you're describing in your question is what Catholic theology calls an *occasion of sin*. In his *Pocket Catholic Dictionary,* Fr. John Hardon, S.J., defines an occasion of sin as "any person, place, or thing that of its nature or because of human frailty can lead one to do wrong, thereby committing sin." We have a moral obligation to avoid occasions of sin because of what they can lead us to.

If you go to wild parties like the ones you describe, you are putting yourself at risk of joining in the bad, sinful behaviors that are taking place. Even if you don't actually fall into sin, you are still silently supporting and giving approval to sin just by being there. Find something better—and more spiritually profitable—to do with your time.

When faced with an occasion of sin, always pray to get yourself out of the situation. Just as in the Lord's Prayer we ask the Father "lead us not into temptation," we must always be on guard against those things that can lead us into danger. Be sure to always make frequent use of the sacraments of reconciliation and the Eucharist which provide us the necessary graces for strengthening our resolve to do what is good and avoid what is evil.

Question #175

"Is smoking a sin? Sure, it's not healthy, but neither is eating fast food."

A. If you are old enough to smoke legally (eighteen years old in most U.S. states) the Church says this is morally permissible if done in moderation. But, of course, it is better not to smoke. Can you imagine Jesus and Mary lighting up a Marlboro and puffing away?

To the degree that smoking is harmful to the body, it is sinful to that degree. Eating is necessary for the body, but some meals are healthier than others. If you had to live on a strict diet of McDonald's and Mississippi River water, you would be able to live. If you had to live on a strict diet of smokes, you would die in a week without food. So, smoking is neither necessary nor beneficial for the body.

No one doubts that smoking lowers your life expectancy, so it is sometimes hard to understand why any person would choose to begin smoking. If you do smoke, it is in your best interest to quit. It could be argued that teens who smoke are not really loving their future spouses or children. Each time they light up, they are probably shortening their time with their future spouse and children. Ask yourself, "Am I willing to one day look into the eyes of my wife or husband as I whisper or cough my last words to her or him, explaining how sorry I am that she or he will have to take care of the kids and die alone, because I sure liked tobacco?" Hopefully, this is a sufficient reason to quit—or avoid smoking altogether.

Question #176

"What does the Church say about body piercing and tattoos?"

A. Though the Church has not issued any formal teaching on this issue, a couple of things should be kept in mind. In traditional Judaism, people who die with tattoos or body piercings are denied burial. This belief comes from Leviticus 19:28: "Do not lacerate your bodies for the dead, and do not tattoo yourselves. I am the LORD." Biblical scholars believe this prohibition was given to keep the Jewish people from following in practices common to the pagan cultures around them. This is why some Christian churches today preach against body piercings and tattoos.

From the Catholic perspective, the Second Vatican Council declared that the human person is obliged to regard the body "as good and honorable since God created it and will raise it up on the last day."[28] Some of the tattoos you see people with today do not look very "good and honorable" and would not be appropriate for someone who is a follower of Jesus.

Remember, our bodies are the temples of the Holy Spirit (1 Cor 6:19-20; CCC 364). We need to respect them as awesome creations of God, reflecting his image and likeness. Though the Church does not forbid women from wearing make-up or earrings, an excessive attachment to one's appearance is vanity and can be sinful.

Also, keep in mind that tattoos will be with you for the rest of your life—unless you go through a painful removal process. What seems like a "cool" tattoo when you are a senior in high school may look pretty silly when you are a parent or grandparent!

Chapter 10
CATHOLIC PRAYER
AND WORSHIP

Question #177

"Did the first Christians celebrate Mass like we do today?"

A. We know from the New Testament that the liturgical celebration eventually called "the Mass" (or simply "Mass") was celebrated from the very beginning of the Church. St. Luke, in the book of the Acts of the Apostles, writes that the early Christians participated in the "breaking of the bread" (see Acts 2:42). St. Paul actually instructs the people of Corinth in the proper reception of the "Lord's supper" (1 Cor 11:20). Other sources tell us that by the end of the first century, the word *Eucharist* (from the Greek word *eucharistia*—"thanksgiving") began to be used regularly to describe the celebration.

The *Catechism* tells us that, "From the beginning the Church has been faithful to the Lord's command. Of the Church of Jerusalem it is written: 'They devoted themselves to the apostles' teaching and fellowship, to the breaking of bread and the prayers ...' From that time on down to our own day the celebration of the Eucharist has been continued, so that today we encounter it everywhere

232 Did Jesus Have a Last Name?

in the Church with the same fundamental structure" (Acts 2:42; CCC 1342–1343).

Though the Mass has undergone a number of variations over the centuries (e.g., the language of the Liturgy being changed from Greek to Latin, and more recently from Latin to modern languages such as English), its essential form has remained unchanged from the time of the first Christians. "From the beginning Christians have celebrated the Eucharist ... in a form whose substance has not changed despite the great diversity of times and liturgies ... because we know ourselves to be bound by the command the Lord gave on the eve of his Passion: 'Do this in remembrance of me'" (CCC 1356).

Question #178

"My teacher says that the Mass is the best prayer we can offer? Is this true?"

A. Your teacher is absolutely right! The Second Vatican Council tells us that, "From the Eucharist, grace is poured forth upon us as from a fountain, and the sanctification of men in Christ and the glorification of God ... No other action of the Church can equal its efficacy by the same title or degree."[29] *Efficacy* simply means usefulness, and thus, the Mass is the most useful and powerful prayer of the Church.

We need to keep in mind what the Mass truly is: the very sacrifice of Jesus on the Cross *re-presented* to us on the altar. Our prayers and intercessions are never more effective than when we unite them to Jesus, perfect Mediator between God the Father and us. In all forms of prayer, we experience a type of communion with God through Jesus. But there can be no greater form of contact with God that is so intimate or so meaningful as the Eucharist. When we receive Jesus through Holy Communion, we are literally receiving the Body, Blood, Soul, and Divinity of the same risen Jesus who walked among us on earth two thousand years ago, but now in sacramental form. In the Eucharist, Jesus comes to dwell within us, becoming one with us and us with him.

There is also a powerful dimension to celebrating the same prayer with millions of people at the same time. Think about it: Catholics across the globe, on every continent, celebrate the Lord's sacrifice in the context of the Mass every day. Some researchers estimate that the Mass is celebrated 300,000 times per day throughout the world! Whenever we go to Mass, we join not only with other Catholics throughout this world, but with the millions of saints and angels in heaven who pray with us during the Liturgy and continually cry, "Holy, Holy, Holy" (Rv 4:8) to the Lamb of God. In this communion of saints, the greatest power source on the planet becomes a reality in our lives.

Question #179

"I am often distracted during Mass, and sometimes I miss what the readings are all about. Is this a sin? And how can I keep this from happening?"

A. Don't feel too badly—you're not the first person to ever become distracted during Mass. Many people struggle with this. Unless you are deliberately thinking about other things or are not trying to pay attention, being distracted is not sinful in itself. However, we need to realize that part of our obligation to attend Mass involves our "full, conscious, and active participation" in it (see CCC 1141).

In order to keep from being distracted during Mass, it helps to keep in mind what we are participating in. As we mentioned in the previous question, the Mass is the very sacrifice of Jesus on the Cross made present to us on the altar. The *Catechism* reminds us that, "In the Eucharist Christ gives us the very blood which he gave up for us on the cross, the very blood which he 'poured out for many for the forgiveness of sins'" (CCC 1365; Mt 26:28). In the Eucharist, we stand at the foot of the Cross with Our Lady, and, like her, unite ourselves with the offering and intercession of Jesus (see CCC 1370).

Here are some practical things you can try: Get to the church ten minutes before the start of Mass to give yourself some time be quiet, to relax, and to get into a reflective mindset. This will help you leave the distractions of life behind and get prepared for the awesome mystery you are about to celebrate. Then, as soon as you get to your seat, kneel in prayer and ask Jesus for the grace to be focused on the words and actions of the Mass. Do not engage in any unnecessary or trivial conversations with your family or friends; talking during Mass is a sure way to be distracted. You may also want to specifically ask St. Teresa of Avila for her intercession, since she struggled with distractions in prayer for many years. Finally, ask the Blessed Mother and all the saints to help you to focus on the Mass as if it were your first time.

Question #180

"Why don't we Catholics use the Bible in our Sunday worship as much as other Christians do?"

A. First of all, we must never forget that the Mass itself is almost entirely biblical. When we break it down and look at its various parts, we see that nearly every word and action is rooted firmly in Sacred Scripture. As we mentioned in a previous answer, a Catholic attending Sunday Mass is exposed to more than seven thousand verses of the Bible per year just from the three Scripture readings presented each week. In addition, all the prayers and responses found within the Mass are scripturally based, at least implicitly. To discover more about the biblical composition of the Mass, I would highly recommend the book *A Biblical Walk Through the Mass.*

It is true that most Catholics do not bring their own Bibles to Mass like many other Christian denominations do in their own Sunday services. Why is this? Part of the answer has to do with the essential difference between Catholic Sunday "services" (i.e., the Mass) and Protestant services. Most Protestant denominations center their Sunday services on the readings from Scripture and the sermon given by the pastor. The Catholic Mass, on the other hand, consists of two fundamental parts: the Liturgy of the Word and the Liturgy of the Eucharist. The essential activity of the Mass is found within the Liturgy of the Eucharist when the priest consecrates the bread and wine and they are transformed into the Body, Blood, Soul, and Divinity of Jesus. We are then invited to come forward and receive Our Lord in Holy Communion.

With all due respect to our Christian friends, no other activity on earth can equal that which takes place during the celebration of the Eucharist during every Mass. As the *Catechism* reminds us, "the Eucharist ... re-presents (makes present) the sacrifice of the cross ... To receive communion is to receive Christ himself who has offered himself for us" (CCC 1366, 1382).

For these reasons, it makes more sense for Catholics to have a missal or missalette available that allows them to follow the entire Order of the Mass. In this way, they receive the full complement of the text for both the Liturgy of the Word and the Liturgy of the Eucharist. In addition to the celebration of the Mass, the Church strongly encourages the study of Sacred Scripture, whether done privately, as a family, or in small-group settings. The important thing to remember is that the actual "book" (the cover, the binding and the pages) is not as important as the *content* of the book (God's Word). As mentioned above, the content of the Bible readings used at Mass are available for everyone to see in the missals provided at Catholic churches, but if you want to bring your own Bible and follow along, that would be a perfectly acceptable thing to do.

Question #181

"Why do we have three readings at Sunday Mass?"

A. The reason we have three readings at Mass on Sundays is because the Church wants us to hear a reading from the Old Testament and two readings from the New Testament (one from the letters of St. Paul and one from the Gospels). This shows us how God's Word is connected, and how the Old Testament is fulfilled in the New Testament.

Many Protestant churches encourage their members to bring their Bibles to church so that they can flip through and mark them up as they listen to the sermon. This not only makes the sermon more interesting, but it also builds one's confidence in using the Bible to learn about and to grow in the Christian Faith.

The Church generally uses missalettes at Mass to allow people to follow along with the readings. But if you want to become more comfortable with the Scriptures, it would also be helpful to bring your Bible with you to church on Sunday. You can look up the three readings for a given Sunday and follow along as they are proclaimed. You may also want to bring a pen and make notes from the homily either in the margins of your Bible or on a notepad. This is a great way to get more actively involved in the Mass—a great step towards the "full, conscious, active participation" we mentioned earlier in this chapter.

Question #182
"What is the holiest day of the year—Easter or Christmas?"

A. This is like asking which wing of a plane does most of the flying, or which of your two eyes is more important.

The answer is that both Easter and Christmas are equally holy. Easter is holy because it celebrates Christ's power over death, the victory he won for us over sin, and gives us a glimpse of our own resurrection. Christmas is holy because it celebrates the birth of our Lord and Savior, Jesus; it honors the day the Second Person of the Trinity came into the world.

Since Easter celebrates the central mystery of our salvation—the resurrection of Jesus from the dead—it is so significant that it cannot be contained within a single day. In the Church's liturgical calendar, the Easter Season is celebrated for fifty days, from Easter Sunday to Pentecost Sunday. In fact, because we celebrate the resurrection of Jesus at every Mass, each Sunday throughout the year could be referred to as a "little Easter."

Remember—it is because Jesus was raised from the dead that we are born to new life as baptized Christians. St.

Paul tells us, "If there is no resurrection then Christ has not been raised; if Christ has not been raised, then our preaching is in vain and our faith is in vain ... But in fact Christ has been raised from the dead, the first fruits of those who have fallen asleep" (1 Cor 15:14, 20). The risen Jesus is the guarantee of our own future resurrection. His life gives meaning to our faith and fuels the fire of hope that we have of spending eternal life with him. Easter is the celebration of our salvation. This is why we rejoice in the words of St. Augustine: "We are Easter people, and Alleluia is our song!"

Question #183

"The Bible says that we should pray in private, but we go to Church with others and also do very visible things like put ashes on our heads. Isn't this a contradiction?"

A. You are referring to the words of Jesus in the Gospel when he instructs us how to pray. As he says, "When you pray, go into your room and shut the door and pray to your Father ... in secret" (Mt 6:6). But we need to understand the context in which Jesus is speaking. In this passage, Jesus is criticizing those "who pray in the synagogues and on the street corners so that others may see them" (Mt 6:5). In other words, Jesus is saying "your reason for praying should not be so that other people think you are a wonderful person and tell you how great you are." If we do this, we're not praying for the right reasons—namely, to worship God for who he is, to thank him for what he has done for us, and to have a real and loving relationship with him.

If we look at the life of Jesus, we see that he constantly prayed to his Father, both privately and publicly. A number of different times in the Gospel, we see Jesus going to a deserted place "by himself to pray" (Mt 14:23). But Jesus also offers many examples of public prayer. As a devout Jew, we know that Jesus shared publicly in the liturgical prayers of the synagogue. When he performed the miracle of the loaves and fishes and fed the five thousand, he looked "up to heaven ... said the blessing, broke the loaves, and gave them to his disciples to set before the people" (Mk 6:41). The Last Supper, in which Jesus instituted the Eucharist, was a public prayer offering to the Father. As St. John describes, during the Last Supper Jesus offered praise and thanksgiving to the Father and prayed for unity among his apostles and their successors who would lead the Church (see Jn 17:1-26).

In a most beautiful way, the *Catechism* tells us that it is "the Holy Spirit in the Church [that] teaches the children of God to pray" (CCC 2661). This is especially true in the Church's public worship, also known as the *liturgy* of the Church. "Prayer internalizes and assimilates the liturgy during and after its celebration. Even when it is lived out 'in secret,' prayer is always prayer *of the Church;* it is a communion with the Holy Trinity" (see Mt 6:6; CCC 2655). In a nutshell, Jesus wants us to be humble and to pray for the right reasons, but he does not want us to keep our faith hidden. So, praying in public in various ways—like saying grace before a meal at a restaurant, or going to a sporting event without washing the ashes off your forehead—can be a good witness for others in society to see.

Question #184

"Why is praying the Rosary important?"

A. It is impossible to describe adequately the profound spiritual benefits of praying the Rosary. This powerful

prayer offers an opportunity for Christians to meditate
on the twenty key events in the lives of Jesus and Mary.
These events are called "mysteries," because we can only
understand a part of their meaning. These twenty mysteries
are divided into five joyful, five sorrowful, five luminous,
and five glorious mysteries, and are prayed on specific days
of the week. Here's an inspiring example of how devotion
to praying the Rosary can work miracles in our lives:

At 8:15 on the morning of August 6, 1945, an atomic bomb
was dropped on Hiroshima, Japan. Within a one-mile
radius of where the bomb was dropped, tens of thousands
died and only four people survived. These four were Jesuit
priests, living only eight blocks from the point at which
the bomb exploded! These priests were missionaries and
prayed the Rosary every day. None of the four was injured
by the radiation. Though all surrounding buildings were
completely destroyed, the parish house remained standing.
If Our Lady can intercede for such extraordinary physical
protection, how much more can she be trusted in other
spiritual matters?

St. John Paul II taught that the Rosary is one of "the
finest and most praiseworthy traditions of Christian
contemplation."[30] While encouraging everyone to pray the
Rosary, the Holy Father made a special plea to families
to take up the practice if they are not already doing so:
"The Holy Rosary, by age-old tradition, has shown itself
particularly effective as a prayer which brings the family
together."[31]

Devotion to Mary is a beautiful—and central—element of
our Faith. The Church rightly honors the Blessed Virgin
with special devotion in the liturgical feasts dedicated to
her and by prayers to her, especially the Rosary. We pray

with and *to* Mary. When we pray to her, asking for her powerful intercession, we are following the will of God the Father who wants us to honor the woman through whom he sent his Son to save humanity (see CCC 971, 2679).

Question #185

"How can Catholics pray the Rosary and think it is a good thing if Jesus condemned repetitious prayer in Matthew 6:7?"

A. A few questions ago, we discussed the two verses right before Matthew 6:7. This is a great illustration of how much depth there is in the Scriptures! Now, if you look closely at this particular verse, Jesus is not condemning the repeating of prayers; he is condemning "vain" repetition, which refers to thinking that God will hear and answer prayers just because of the many words used rather than because of the sincerity of one's heart. It was common during Jesus' time for people to recite lengthy prayers without really loving God or wanting to do his will. Just as some people today struggle with paying attention during Mass or when saying the Rosary, there were many people of Jesus' time who just "went through the motions" without ever having a true conversion of heart. And there were others who invoked pagan gods under dozens of different names in hopes that one of the gods would respond to one of the titles.

We know repetitious prayer, in itself, is *not* displeasing to the Lord. After all, God himself inspired Psalm 136, which repeats the words, "For his steadfast love endures forever" more than twenty-five times! This psalm is much like the prayers of the Rosary: one verse is repeated over and over, while different parts of Israel's redemption and God's mercy are recalled between each. The Rosary is prayed in a similar manner; our minds are lifted to meditate on our redemption and God's mercy, while repeating certain prayers.

According to Revelation 4:8, even the angels in heaven repeat the same prayer ("holy, holy, holy...") for all eternity. And Jesus himself repeats the same prayer three times during his agony in the Garden (see Mt 26:39-44). So, as long as one's heart is offered to God, repetition is not displeasing to him, especially since meditation on the mysteries of Christ's life can hardly be considered vain prayer.

Question #186

"Do we really get grace by sitting in front of the Eucharist during Adoration?"

A. Yes, we do! Eucharistic Adoration is a powerful form of prayer. In Adoration, we don't have to be too concerned about what to say or do. The *Catechism* teaches us that, "In prayer, the faithful God's initiative of love always comes first; our own first step is always a response" (CCC 2567). St. Thérèse of Lisieux described prayer as a "surge of the heart ... a simple look toward heaven."[32] In this way, prayer becomes not something we are initiating, but our response to the grace of God already at work in our hearts.

The power of prayer and the good it does for us becomes especially strengthened when we are in the presence of the Eucharist, especially when we receive Holy Communion. Throughout its history, the Church has encouraged the faithful to extend the reverence given to Jesus in the Eucharist, even beyond the celebration of the Mass. The next best thing to actually receiving Jesus in the Eucharist is to spend time adoring him in the Eucharist, either *reposed* (that is, within the tabernacle) or during exposition of the Blessed Sacrament on the altar.

In the words of John Paul II, "The Church and the world have a great need for Eucharistic worship. Jesus awaits us in this sacrament of love. Let us not refuse the time to go to meet him in adoration ... let our adoration never cease."[33] And Pope Paul VI teaches that "anyone who approaches this ... sacrament with special devotion ... experiences how great is the value of communing with Christ ... for there is nothing more effective for advancing on the road to holiness."[34] The Church draws its life from the Eucharist,[35] and as members of the Church, we can draw life from the Eucharist through time spent adoring Jesus in the Blessed Sacrament.

Question #187

"I went to a Catholic charismatic conference and saw people speaking in tongues, including the priest who was leading the service. They were also doing something called 'slaying people in the spirit.' Are we allowed to do this as Catholics?"

A. The *Catechism* defines a *charism* as "a special gift or grace of the Holy Spirit which directly or indirectly benefits the Church, given in order to help a person live out the Christian life, or to serve the common good in building up the Church" (CCC glossary). One of these special graces is the *gift of tongues,* of which the New Testament mentions two types. The first we know from the Acts of the Apostles: on the day of Pentecost, devout Jews from many nations were able to understand the preaching of the apostles in their own particular language (see Acts 2:1-41). St. Paul, writing in his first letter to the Corinthians, discusses a different kind of gift of tongues: a Christian who speaks in a way that *cannot* be understood. This is also called *glossolalia* (or "speaking in a [foreign] language"). St. Paul explains that this is because the person "who speaks in a tongue speaks not to men but to God; for no one understands him, but he utters mysteries in the Spirit" (1 Cor 14:2).

In the same letter, St. Paul is quick to point out that the gift of tongues is only one of many special gifts of the Spirit and may be considered less important than others. He further states that not everyone receives the same gifts but each person has only what God has given him, all for the building up of the Church (see 1 Cor 12:11, 14:3). So we should never judge a person's holiness or spiritual piety based upon what spiritual gifts he or she possesses. These gifts are given to us from God's goodness, not because someone is more special or better than others.

Today, there is a lot of discussion about the growing charismatic and pentecostal movements within the Church. There is no doubt that God continues to bless his Church with abundant gifts, including the gift of tongues. At certain events, some people may appear to be speaking in tongues. However, we need to be careful in how we evaluate such phenomena. St. Paul tells the people of Corinth that the gift of tongues should be for the benefit of all—not just the speaker. So it is good if the speaker, or someone else, possesses the gift of *interpreting* tongues (that is, the ability to explain the meaning of what is being said). "Therefore he who speaks in a tongue should pray for the power to interpret" (1 Cor 14:13).

The expression "slain in the spirit" (also called "falling in the spirit" or "resting in the spirit") is not directly connected to the charism of speaking in tongues. It usually occurs when someone falls to the floor while being prayed over by someone else, usually with the laying on of hands. People who have had such an experience often report a feeling of tremendous joy and peace, and they may even begin to cry over feeling deep remorse for their past sins. Some cry tears of joy as they realize the hope found in Christ. Others may even experience some form of physical or spiritual healing. Such a phenomenon is highly unusual; it should judged in light of the spiritual benefits it gives to both the person "slain" and to others in the Church.

Question #188

"What good does fasting do? Why would denying myself food or meat help me get closer to God?"

A. From the earliest period of the Church's history, Christians have taken up the practice of fasting, particularly during the season of Lent. The *Catechism* defines fasting as, "refraining from food and drink as an expression of interior penance ... in imitation of the fast of Jesus for forty days in the desert. Fasting ... is recommended in Scripture and the writings of the Church Fathers" (CCC glossary).

In his book *Straight Answers: Answers to 100 Questions about the Faith* (Cathedral Press, 1998), Fr. William Saunders points out that St. Paul reminds us how, "'Continually we carry about in our bodies the dying of Jesus, so that in our bodies the life of Jesus may also be revealed' (2 Corinthians 4:10). We too are charged to convert our whole lives—body and soul—to the Lord. This conversion process involves doing penance, including bodily mortification (the disciplining and self-denial of the body and its appetites) like fasting, for our sins and weaknesses, which in turn strengthens and heals us."[36]

The Church encourages us in the practice of fasting and teaches that the interior penance of the Christian can be expressed in many and various ways. In addition to fasting, Scripture and the Church Fathers insist above all on two additional forms, *prayer* and *almsgiving* (i.e., giving to the poor), which express our conversion in relation to ourselves, to God, and to one another. Combined with fasting, prayer and almsgiving help us in our spiritual journey by bringing us closer to Jesus, who personally sacrificed so much for us.

Question #189

"How can I explain to my non-Catholic friend that the Catholic practice of observing holy days of obligation does not contradict the Bible? Where does the Bible say that the Church has the authority to establish these days?"

A. We see in the book of Acts that the early Christians celebrated the Lord's Day (see Acts 20:7), which was Sunday. By having holy days, the Church has, in effect, simply said, "If we can celebrate Jesus' resurrection, let's celebrate his incarnation, his passion, his transfiguration ... In fact, let's also celebrate his entire life all year long so that our lives become a continual meditation on the mysteries of his life." The authority to establish these feast days was given to the Church by Jesus.

Where is that in the Bible? Look at Matthew 16:19 and 18:18. In these passages, Jesus told the Church leaders, "Whatever you bind on earth will be bound in heaven, and whatever you loose on earth will be loosed in heaven." This language of *binding* and *loosing* was known by the Jews as the ability to establish rules for a faith community. Included in this authority was forbidding (and permitting) certain actions—for example, establishing days of fasting. In the Gospel of Matthew, we read about the scribes and Pharisees who "bind heavy burdens and lay them on men's shoulders," but will not "move them [loose them] with their finger" (Mt 23:2-4). Just as the Jewish leaders once had authority over the feast days, Jesus Christ gave this authority to his Church.

But the Church is not merely a kingdom with rules. It is better understood as God's family. In each family, parents have the authority to establish devotions. So, if the father decides that everyone will pray the Rosary after dinner, he has the right to make this a family obligation. Similarly, the Church establishes devotions and holy days of obligation for the sake of the children of God—for our own spiritual good.

Chapter 11

MISCELLANEOUS
QUESTIONS

Question #190

"Did Jesus tell us not to eat meat on Fridays during Lent, or is this practice something the Church created?"

A. Many non-Catholics don't understand the Catholic practice of abstaining from meat during the Fridays of Lent. Even some Catholics wonder about it. How does not eating meat one day a week help us grow closer to Jesus or become holier?

It is true that Jesus did not explicitly teach in Scripture that we should abstain from meat on Fridays during Lent, but we need to remember that he did speak about the good that can come from fasting. In Matthew 4:21, we read about how Jesus fasted for forty days and nights in preparation for his public ministry, and he gives the apostles instructions on how to fast for the sake of God's kingdom (see Mt 6:16-18). He also established the Church to guide his people in the Christian life. Jesus gave the apostles—and their successors, the bishops—the authority to "bind" and "loose" (see Mt 16:18), that is, to establish discipline and practices for the spiritual well-being of his followers.

Since we all suffer the effects of original sin and often commit personal sins, we need to be purified from our self-will so we can do God's will. This is the process of *conversion*. Both the Bible and the Fathers of the Church teach that there are three sure-fire ways our conversion to Christ can be strengthened: prayer, *fasting*, and almsgiving (see CCC 1434). It is not that there is anything morally wrong with eating meat. But following a spiritual discipline, like fasting, can have a powerful effect of purification on us personally and on the Church as an entity. The Church's call for us to abstain from meat is a wonderful way that we—as a truly Catholic and universal community—recognize our need for Christ, repent of our sins, and go deeper in our conversions *together.*

If we deliberately ignore the Church's disciplinary laws—such as those relating to fasting and abstinence from meat—this is really a rejection of the Church and its authority, which is a grave sin. Jesus said to his apostles, "He who hears you, hears me; whoever rejects you, rejects me" (Lk 10:16). So if we rebel against the teaching authority of the Church, we are rebelling against Jesus himself.

Question #191

"What about eating meat on Fridays outside of Lent?"

A. Officially, Catholics throughout the world are still asked to abstain from meat on *all* Fridays throughout the year, unless the episcopal conferences (that is, all the bishops) in a particular country or region substitute another form of penance.

There was some confusion about this issue after the Second Vatican Council ended in 1965. To clear up this confusion, Pope Paul VI issued a decree stating that the traditional practice of abstaining from meat on Fridays was to continue, but gave the bishops of each country the right to make their own law.[37] In 1966, the Catholic bishops of the United States decided to make abstinence from meat optional on Fridays outside of Lent.

But they stated that while the *requirement* to abstain from meat is no longer in place, it is highly recommended that the faithful continue this time-honored practice, or some other forms of self-denial and penance. So, even though it is not a sin to eat meat on Fridays outside of Lent, we are still required to do some form of penance or an act of charity in its place.

Abstaining from meat—and fasting in general—has been a common practice since the earliest days of the Church. From the very first century, the day of the week on which Christ died, Friday, traditionally has been observed as a day of abstaining from meat. Such acts of penance help join us closer to Jesus and remind us of the sufferings that he endured for our salvation. Whatever type of penance or work of charity we do, this sacrifice helps make reparation for our past sins and helps us grow in holiness.

Question #192

"Since eating meat on Friday is not a sin anymore, are there people still in hell for eating meat when it was a sin?"

A. First, a few words about hell. The poor souls in hell are there for all eternity; there is no getting out early for "good behavior" (CCC 1035). The Church has always taught that our eternal resting place (either heaven or hell) is determined by our own free choice (see CCC 1036–1037). Remember—God cannot force us to love him; we either *choose* to love him or not. But we do not love God if we sin mortally against him, against our neighbor, or against ourselves. If we die in mortal sin without repenting and without asking for God's merciful forgiveness, we have *chosen* to be separated from him forever.

This being said, we must never assume that a particular person is in hell, because it is impossible for us to know the state of a person's soul at the hour of death. Only God knows this. We should always hope and pray that every person, prior to death, implores God's mercy and seeks forgiveness for their sins. This is why the regular reception of the sacraments—especially the Holy Eucharist and penance—is so important in helping us to be prepared for our death, whenever it may come.

Though the Church's laws on fasting and abstinence have undergone some changes over the years, our accountability in following these laws has not changed. For example, we know that the Church still requires Catholics to abstain from eating meat on Ash Wednesday and on Fridays during Lent. A Catholic who fails to abstain from eating meat on a Friday during Lent is not necessarily committing a serious sin. But if a Catholic is fully aware of the Church's law and deliberately chooses to break this law, he or she is at least in danger of having committed a mortal sin.

Of course, Catholics in the past who deliberately disregarded the Church's law were also likely committing grave sin. And, as the Church teaches, "the souls of those who die in a state of mortal sin descend into hell" (CCC 1035). This might sound harsh—after all, it was just a piece of meat, right? Why should eating meat send someone to hell? But remember, it is not the meat that is sinful. Rather, it is disobeying the legitimate authority of the Church that is sinful. Why? Jesus told his apostles, the leaders of the Church, "Whoever rejects you rejects me" (Lk 10:16). Rejecting the Church's desire for us to fast is, in effect, telling Christ that we do not want to follow him in all ways; we would rather just follow him when it is convenient. It is this attitude of rebellion and this type of selfish decision that creates such a grave matter through which someone could place their soul into the jeopardy of mortal sin.

Question #193

"What do guardian angels do?"

A. Throughout the Bible, there are many accounts of guardian angels providing help and protection to humans. In the life of Jesus, we read about angels protecting him as an infant, serving him in the desert, and strengthening him during his agony in the garden (see Mt 1:20, 2:13, 19; 4:11; 26:53; Mk 1:13; Lk 22:43; CCC 333). In the Acts of the Apostles, when Peter was miraculously set free from prison and his friends could not believe it, they commented that the person at the door could not be Peter but that "it must be his angel" (Acts 12:15).

Because our guardian angels are so close to us, we are encouraged to pray to them for their constant intercession and protection in helping lead us to heaven. One of the most treasured prayers recited by children and people of all ages is the prayer that we can each pray to our guardian angel: "Angel of God, my guardian dear, to whom God's love entrusts me here: Ever this day be at my side, to light, to guard, to rule and guide."

Question #194

"Do people who were never baptized have guardian angels?"

A. This is an excellent question. Many theologians hold that every human being, whether baptized or not, has a guardian angel. Jesus himself clearly makes reference to them in the Gospel when he warns against those who would attempt to lead children into sin: "See that you do not despise one of these little ones, for I say to you that their angels in heaven always look upon the face of my heavenly father" (Mt 18:10). Notice he does not say "*baptized* children."

In Psalm 91:11-12, there is a mention of guardian angels before baptism existed: "For God commands the angels to guard you in all your ways. With their hands they shall support you, lest you strike your foot against a stone." Since God gave guardian angels to those who were not baptized back then, it would certainly make sense that he would do the same now.

Question #195

"Do our guardian angels get a new 'assignment' after we die?"

A. This is one of the few "we don't know" answers in this book. The Church has not taught anything on this subject, so theologians are free to speculate. Because each individual person is unique and "unrepeatable," it would seem appropriate that guardian angels are not "recycled" and given to another person.

On a slightly different note, there are people who sometimes pray that their guardian angel will go help someone else in need, such as when they have a family member who is in a dangerous situation. In this case, if the guardian angel were to honor this request and evacuate his first assignment temporarily in order to give some support to another guardian angel having a particularly rough day with his assignment, then maybe that could be considered to be a sort of angelic maneuvering among assignments!

Question #196

"Can angels read our minds?"

A. Because angelic minds are very powerful, they possess an extraordinary ability that enables them to perceive intuitively what we may be thinking based upon our actions, words, or personality. This is similar to the way a human being who knows you extremely well can sometimes be said to "know what you're thinking." But that's not really mind-reading. Only God can know with certainty the thoughts that are exclusively our own. So, strictly speaking, only God can read our minds. To accomplish his will, God may sometimes enable a creature—such as an angel or a saint—to know our thoughts in a particular matter, but this is an exception.

This then begs the question, "How can Satan plant ideas or temptations in our minds if he doesn't know what we're thinking?" As we said above, his angelic intellect has a very strong intuitive sense about what we are thinking without actually being able to read our minds. Just like someone can whisper a suggestion in our ears, so Satan can tempt us in a similar way.

Question #197

"Do you think the Ark of the Covenant or Noah's Ark will ever be found?"

A. Some people certainly think so. An expedition took place in the summer of 2004 to explore a mountainous region in Turkey where many people claim the remains of Noah's Ark can be found. A joint team of Americans and Turks climbed Mount Ararat, located on the eastern border of Turkey next to Armenia, to a site where satellite images have helped pinpoint the exact location where they think the Ark may rest. Their findings were inconclusive.

Over the years, many people have speculated on the possibility of the remains of Noah's Ark being found in this same region. As we mentioned in the answer to question 35, the Bible itself mentions how Noah's Ark "came to rest on the mountains of Ararat" (Gn 8:4). We also discussed how a number of prominent people have written about the location of the Ark over the centuries, and that others have explored the same area or flown over the supposed site and taken photographs. Whether or not the remains of Noah's Ark can be found there (or in any other place) after all the centuries that have passed is an open question.

Regarding the Ark of the Covenant, history records nothing of it after the year 587 BC when the Babylonians burned and destroyed Jerusalem, taking the Israelites as captives with them. The period that immediately followed this is known as the "Babylonian Exile" or the "Babylonian Captivity." Whether the Ark of the Covenant was also seized and carried with them to Babylon is not mentioned in the scriptural account (see 2 Kgs 25:13-17). As you may recall, the Ark of the Covenant was a wooden box covered in gold with two cherub angels with outstretched wings on the lid (all of which was prescribed by God to Moses in Exodus 25:10-22). The box was roughly 45 inches long (2.5 cubits) and 27 inches wide (1.5 cubits) and high (1.5 cubits). Within the box were carried the two tablets of the Ten Commandments, given by God to Moses on Mount

Sinai. This is where the presence of God was known to reside, which the Israelites carried with them as they migrated throughout the wilderness.

Eventually, the Ark was placed in the Holy of Holies, the sanctuary within the great Temple of Jerusalem built by King Solomon (see 1 Kgs 8:1-9). There it is thought to have remained until the Temple was destroyed by the Babylonians in 587 BC. What became of the Ark after that is anyone's guess.

The speculation surrounding this mystery has led to a number of theories and has even inspired the making of Steven Spielberg's blockbuster 1981 movie *Raiders of the Lost Ark,* starring Harrison Ford as Indiana Jones. Aside from what Hollywood thinks might have happened to it, one of the most interesting theories involves a small chapel in Ethiopia.

This theory involves the Queen of Sheba who, as mentioned in the Bible, visited King Solomon (see 1 Kgs 10). Most scholars agree that the queen came from a region known today as part of the country of Yemen. Others, however, have argued she came from the present-day country of Ethiopia, a neighbor of Yemen. According to Ethiopian legend, the queen had a son whose father was King Solomon. The son's name was Menelik, who is said to have visited King Solomon himself whereupon some of his aides stole the Ark and brought it back to what is present-day Ethiopia. From there, the Ark was thought to have been kept in various locations until it was finally placed within the St. Mary of Zion Chapel in the town of Axum, Ethiopia. According to the claim by many Ethiopian Orthodox Christians, it is within this chapel that the Ark of the Covenant is presently located. Whether this is true or not, we don't know for sure, but it certainly makes for an interesting story and may even provide a great opportunity for a school research project (stop groaning)!

Question #198

"I know that many Christians are against celebrating Halloween, saying it is a pagan holiday. Does the Catholic Church have a position on the celebration of Halloween?"

A. It is true that historical evidence shows that Halloween *is* rooted in an ancient pagan custom. On the night of October 31 (and continuing into November 1), the Celts of Ireland annually celebrated the end of their harvest and gave tribute to *Samhain,* the "god of the dead." It was believed that on this feast, the worlds of the living and the dead touched one another and that the spirits of those who died the previous year went searching for living bodies to possess. Of course, the people of the villages didn't want to be possessed, so they dressed up in costumes to scare the spirits away. As the Celts were converted to Christianity, these customs became ceremonial and cultural rather than religious. In the 1840s, when millions of Irish immigrated to the United States, they brought many of their Halloween customs with them.

By the time of Christ, the Jewish faith had fairly well-developed beliefs regarding the afterlife, and the practice of praying for the dead had became common (see 2 Macc 12:38-46). In the early Church, the anniversary of a martyr's death was celebrated with a Mass, and stories of the saint's life were told and his memory honored. This honor soon came to be given to *all* holy Christian men and women who had passed away.

When Christianity encountered pagan feasts in the Roman Empire, it would routinely replace them with Christian feasts by "baptizing" them and incorporating them into the life of the Church. Some have argued that this shows the pagan roots of Christianity, but this is simply false. The Church *intentionally* placed Christian celebrations directly onto pagan holidays, precisely to show the victory of Christianity over paganism! Such is the case with Halloween.

By the ninth century, after Christianity had spread to Britain and Ireland and encountered the Celtic celebration of Samhain, All Saints Day was established on November 1 as an annual feast of the Church. Thus, the informal "baptism" of the feast of Samhain began. The night before All Saints Day became known as *All Hallow's Eve,* which became shortened into "Halloween."

Since then, Halloween has become a secular holiday in our culture, but one that recently seems to have reverted back to its pagan roots by focusing on the "dark side" of spiritual things. We see this as more kids dress up as demons or ax murderers than they do as saints or even superheroes. Many Christians are disturbed by this trend and, as a result, no longer celebrate Halloween. While their view is to be respected, there's another option— to follow the lead of the early Church and "re-baptize" Halloween! Some suggestions: Pass out candy with a Scripture verse tied to it; dress up as saints (rather than demons); tell the trick-or-treaters that Jesus loves them; if you're really into the bloody costumes, then dress up as one of the martyrs; research their whole story, and then use it as an opportunity to evangelize when people ask who you are supposed to be! As St. Paul states in his first letter to the Corinthians, "I have become all things to all men, that I may by all means save some" (1 Cor 9:22).

Question #199

"Can Catholics be cremated?"

A. Yes. But the *Code of Canon Law,* the official law of the Church, recommends that Catholics choose traditional burial.[38] This is because the body is "the temple of the Holy Spirit" prior to death (see 1 Cor 6:19), and also because it is more appropriate for a Christian to follow the example of Jesus' own burial. Nonetheless, the Church does allow cremation, as long as it is not chosen for reasons contrary to Christian teaching. Such reasons would include hatred of the Catholic Church or denial of the doctrine of the resurrection of the body (see CCC 2301). It is recommended—though not required—that cremation should take place *after* a funeral Mass.

Question #200

"Why isn't Joseph, the husband of Mary, mentioned that much in the Bible?"

A. A big part of the answer has to do with the fact that little is mentioned in the Bible about the first thirty years of Jesus' earthly life. Most of the Gospel focuses on the three years of Jesus' public ministry, and his subsequent journey to Jerusalem where he would suffer and die for our sins and be resurrected on the third day.

Joseph is mentioned in the genealogy at the beginning of Matthew's Gospel (Mt 1:1-17) and in the infancy narratives in both Matthew and Luke (see Mt 1, 2; Lk 1, 2). You think your dreams are weird? In these two Gospels, we read about Joseph's dreams: how he received messages from an angel to take Mary as his wife, to flee to Egypt to save the infant Jesus from King Herod's decision to kill all firstborn sons, and to return safely to Nazareth after Herod had died (see Mt 1:18-24, 2:13-23). We also read how Joseph accompanied Mary to present Jesus in the Temple forty days after his birth, according to Jewish law (see Lk 2:22-38). The last time Joseph is specifically mentioned in the Bible is when he and Mary are in Jerusalem for Passover and became separated from the twelve-year-old Jesus. They search for him for three days, eventually finding him teaching in the Temple (Lk 2:41-51). Aside from these few passages, the Bible makes only passing references to Joseph, mostly when speaking of Jesus as "the carpenter's son."

Because it was common in those days for a man in his twenties (or older) to marry a teenage girl, Joseph was probably much older than Mary. Most scholars speculate that he is not mentioned more in the Bible because he had already died before Jesus began his public ministry. Though Mary and other relatives of Jesus are mentioned a number of times, Joseph is not. At the crucifixion, Jesus hands care of his mother, Mary, to the apostle John, indicating that Joseph was not alive at this time to care for her himself (Jn 19:26-27).

In the beautiful tradition of the Church, St. Joseph is the patron saint of a happy death. We can easily picture St. Joseph on his deathbed, Our Lady standing on one side holding his hand and Jesus holding his other. Pray to St. Joseph for the grace to live a life as a faithful follower of Jesus and be filled with joy and peace every day until God calls you home to be with him forever.

Notes

1 St. Thomas Aquinas, *Summa Theologiae* I, 2, 3.
2 St. Ambrose, *De Sacramentis,* 5, 4, 30.
3 St. Thomas Aquinas, *Summa Theologiae* III, 1, 3.
4 If you want to read more about this very interesting research, check out the article "Mitochondrial DNA and Human Evolution," in the journal *Nature*—available online in their archive section: 1 January 1987; 325 (6099); 1-92.
5 St. Thomas Aquinas, *De Malo* 4, 1.
6 Second Vatican Council, Dogmatic Constitution on the Church, *Lumen Gentium* 1 (1964).
7 Second Vatican Council, Dogmatic Constitution on Divine Revelation, *Dei Verbum* 11 (1965); emphasis added.
8 Flavius Josephus, *Antiquities of the Jews*, XX, ii, 2.
9 Marco Polo, *The Travels of Marco Polo.*
10 For more information on the Shroud, an excellent book is Dr. Gilbert Lavoie's *Unlocking the Secrets of the Shroud* (Thomas More, 1998). He suggests that the image on the Shroud may have been formed at the very moment of the Resurrection. You may also want to check out the video *Silent Witness* (Holy Shroud Guild, 1979), which demonstrates some of the science used in studying the Shroud, as well as some of the intriguing discoveries made about it.
11 St. Ignatius of Antioch, *Letter to the Smyrneans* 8, 2.
12 St. Cyprian, *De Unitate* 6.
13 *New York Times* editorial, December 25, 1941.
14 As quoted by Fr. William Saunders in the *Arlington Catholic Herald*, April 14, 1994).
15 G.K. Chesterton, *Autobiography*, Collected Works, Vol. 16, 212.
16 *Code of Canon Law* (CIC), no. 844.
17 St. Justin Martyr, *Apologia*, 1, 65.
18 St. Teresa, *Life*, 8, 5.
19 Second Vatican Council, Dogmatic Constitution of the Church, *Lumen Gentium* 16 (1964).

20 *CIC*, no. 1031.

21 *CIC*, no. 643.

22 John Paul II, *Ordinatio Sacerdotalis* 4 (1994). In this important encyclical letter, "The Ordination of Priests," the pope clearly explains why only men can be ordained to the priesthood.

23 St. John of the Cross, *Dichos* 64.

24 Martin Luther, from his sermon "On the Day of the Conception of the Mother of God," given December 1527; from the book *Luther,* Hartmann Grisar, S.J.

25 American Cancer Society, "Human Papilloma Virus," (2002). Cancer.org

26 Fr. Frank Pavone, article *Rape and Abortion*, published Sept. 8, 1998.

27 See Pope John Paul II, *Evangelium Vitae* 56 (1995). In this encyclical letter, "The Gospel of Life," the pope discusses the death penalty. He points our that as long as our penal system is "sufficient to defend human life against an aggressor and to protect public order and the safety of persons, public authority must limit itself to [punishments other than the death penalty] because they better correspond to the concrete conditions of the common good and are more in conformity to the dignity of the human person."

28 Second Vatican Council, Pastoral Constitution on the Church in the Modern World, *Gaudium et Spes* 14 (1965).

29 Second Vatican Council, Dogmatic Constitution on the Liturgy, *Sancrosanctum Concilium* 7, 10 (1963).

30 John Paul II, *Rosarium Virginis Mariae* 5, "On the Rosary of the Virgin Mary."

31 John Paul II, *Rosarium Virginis Mariae* 41, "On the Rosary of the Virgin Mary."

32 St. Therésè of Lisieux, *Manuscrits autobiographiques,* C 25r.

33 John Paul II, *Dominicae Cenae* 3 (1980).

34 Pope Paul VI, *Mysterium Fidei* 1.67 (1965).

35 See John Paul II, *Ecclesia de Eucharistia* 1 (2003).

36 Saunders, 94.

37 Pope Paul VI, Apostolic Constitution on Penance, *Poenitemini* (1966).

38 CIC, no. 1176.

Acknowledgments

Many thanks to Joseph Lewis and Brian Butler for their dedication to the project over the course of several years of development, and whose creative contributions helped improve many of the answers; to Michael J. Miller, Paul Thigpen, Ph.D., Christopher Cope, Jennifer Cope, Michael Flickinger, Michael Fontecchio, and Elena Perri for their editorial and technical assistance; and to Kinsey Caruth, for yet another creative cover.

Resources

Here is a list of apostolates, magazines, books, and encyclicals that can provide you with more information on the topics contained in this book:

Apostolates and Institutions

Courage, 210 W. 31st Street, New York, NY 10001. Website: Courage.org. Founded by Fr. John Harvey, O.S.F.S., this ministry offers support to the Catholics with a homosexual orientation who are striving to live chaste lives.

Real Love, Inc., 191 University Blvd., #335, Denver, CO 80206. Phone: (303) 237-7942. Website: RealLove.net. Apostolate founded by Mary Beth Bonacci dedicated to promoting chastity and a pro-life and pro-family message through seminars, tracts, books, and tapes.

St. Joseph Communications, P.O. Box 1911, Suite 83, Tehachapi, CA 93581. Phone: (800) 526–2151. Website: SaintJoe.com. Publishes audio by Dr. Scott Hahn, Kimberly Hahn, Bishop Fulton Sheen, Jeff Cavins, Jesse Romero, and many others.

National Association for Research and Therapy of Homosexuality (NARTH) – Thomas Aquinas Psychological Clinic, 16633 Ventura Blvd., Suite 1340, Encino, CA 91436. Phone: (818) 789-4440. Website: Narth.com. Assists the person with a homosexual orientation to rediscover his or her true heterosexual identity using reparative therapy.

Authors

Chesterton, G. K. — The works of G. K. Chesterton can be found at Chesterton.org or by writing The American Chesterton Society, 4117 Pebblebrook Circle, Minneapolis, MN 55437. Phone: (952) 831-3096.

Lewis, C. S. — The works of C.S. Lewis can be found at cslewis.org or by writing the C.S. Lewis Foundation, P.O. Box 8008, Redlands, CA 92375. Phone: 1-888-CSLEWIS.

Sheed, Frank — Books by Frank Sheed are available through various publishers.

Books and Booklets

100 Answers to Your Questions on Annulments, Edward N. Peters, J.C.D., J.D., 1997, 2004. Ascension Press, P.O. Box 1990, West Chester, PA 19380.

Answering Jehovah's Witnesses, Jason Evert, 2001. Catholic Answers, 2020 Gillespie Way, El Cajon, CA 92020.

The Bible and the Catholic Church, Fr. Peter Stravinskas, 1996. Ignatius Press, 2515 McAllister St., San Francisco, CA 94118.

The Catechism of the Catholic Church, 1994. Doubleday, 1745 Broadway, New York, NY 10019.

Darwin on Trial, Phillip E. Johnson, 1993. InterVarsity Press, P.O. Box 1400, Downers Grove, IL 60515.

Darwin's Black Box, Michael J. Behe, 1996. The Free Press, 1230 Avenue of the Americas, New York, NY.

The Faith, Fr. John Hardon, S.J., 1995. Servant Books, Box 8617, Ann Arbor, MI 48107.

Healing the Homosexual, Dr. Joseph Nicolosi. Write or call: 16633 Ventura Blvd., Suite 1340, Encino, CA 91436.

The Homosexual Person, Father John Harvey, 1987. Ignatius Press, 2515 McAllister St., San Francisco, CA 94118.

How the Bible Has Come To Us, J. M. Casciaro and J. L. Navarro, Scepter Press, P.O. Box 211, 8W 38th St. Suite 802, New York, NY 10018.

If You Really Love Me, Jason Evert, 1999. Catholic Answers, 2020 Gillespie Way, El Cajon, CA 92020.

Inside Islam: A Guide for Catholics, Daniel Ali & Robert Spencer, 2003. Ascension Press, P.O. Box 1990, West Chester, PA 19380.

Real Love, Mary Beth Bonacci, 1996. Ignatius Press, 2515 McAllister St., San Francisco, CA 94118.

A Short History of the Catholic Church, Jose Orlandis. Catholic Answers, 2020 Gillespie Way, El Cajon, CA 92020.

Theology for Beginners, Frank J. Sheed, 1958, 1976. Servant Books, Box 8617, Ann Arbor, MI 48107.

Theology of the Body for Beginners, Christopher West, 2004. Ascension Press, P.O. Box 1990, West Chester, PA 19380.

The Truth About Homosexuality, Father John Harvey, 1996. Ignatius Press, 2515 McAllister St., San Francisco, CA 94118.

Triumph: The Power and the Glory of the Catholic Church: A 2,000 Year History, Harry W. Crocker III, 2001. Prima Publishing, Roseville, CA.

Where We Got the Bible, Rev. Henry Graham. Catholic Answers, 2020 Gillespie Way, El Cajon, CA 92020.

Why Wait?, Josh McDowell and Dick Day, 1994. Here's Life Publishers, P.O. Box 1576, San Bernardino, CA 92402.

Magazine

Envoy, P.O. Box 640, Granville, OH.

Encyclicals, Papal Letters, and Declarations

Evangelium Vitae (The Gospel of Life), John Paul II, 1995.

Humanae Vitae (Of Human Life), Paul VI, 1968.

On the Pastoral Care of Homosexual Persons, Congregation for the Doctrine of the Faith, 1986.

Ordinatio Sacredotalis (Apostolic Letter Reserving the Priesthood to Men), John Paul II, 1994.

Women: Teachers of Peace, John Paul II, 1995.

Papal documents can be found at NewAdvent.org or EWTN.com. Printed copies can be purchased through the Daughters of St. Paul, 50 St. Paul's Ave., Boston, MA 02130. Pauline.org

Index

Topic/Question

Topic/Question